GOODNESS AND MERCY
SHALL FOLLOW ME

GOODNESS *and* MERCY SHALL FOLLOW ME

*A Memoir of Old Jerusalem
by Avraham Frank*

Translated by
NEHAMA STAMPFER GLOGOWER

LUMINARE PRESS
WWW.LUMINAREPRESS.COM

Goodness and Mercy Shall Follow Me: A Memoir of Old Jerusalem
Copyright © 2024 by Dani Yardeni

All rights reserved. This book or any portion thereof may not be reproduced or used in any manner whatsoever without the express written permission of the publisher, except for the use of brief quotations in a book review.

Printed in the United States of America

Luminare Press
442 Charnelton St.
Eugene, OR 97401
www.luminarepress.com

LCCN: 2023909241
ISBN: 979-8-88679-209-6

This translation was a labor of love, but getting it published required additional resources. I'd like to thank the following sponsors towards the publication:

Zvi Brian Lando, son of David Lando, z"l, grandson of Minah Lando

Dov Steven Lando, son of David Lando, z"l, grandson of Minah Lando

Yehudah Lando, son of Minah Lando

Avivah Litan, daughter of Ida, granddaughter of Channah Sachs

Shaul Stampfer, son of Joshua Stampfer, grandson of Nechama Stampfer

Meir Stampfer, son of Joshua Stampfer, grandson of Nechama Stampfer

Elana Emlen, daughter of Joshua Stampfer, granddaughter of Nechama Stampfer

I also wish to acknowledge the estate of Rabbi Joshua and Goldie Stampfer, my dear parents, who continue to inspire me.

Contents

Translator's Introduction 1
Foreword 7
Preface 11

    CHAPTER ONE
    These are the Generations 15

    CHAPTER TWO
    My Childhood in Jerusalem 52

    CHAPTER THREE
    Growing Up 98

    CHAPTER FOUR
    Malkah Joins 126

    CHAPTER FIVE
    Leaving Jerusalem 138

    CHAPTER SIX
    The Techno-Kefitz Plant and "A Lively
    Inanimate Object" 149

    CHAPTER SEVEN
    May the Memory of the Righteous
    be a Blessing 161

    CHAPTER EIGHT
    My Brothers and Sisters 168

    CHAPTER NINE
    My Uncle, Rabbi Aryeh Levin 194

Bibliography 201

TRIBUTES TO AVRAHAM FRANK

Elyakim Rubenstein 203

Rabbi David HaCohen 209

Shaul Stampfer 213

Rabbi Shabbetai Rosenthal 219

Zehava Bazak 222

Raffi Frank 229

Gitti Yardeni 237

Glossary 241

Translator's Introduction

I grew up on the opposite side of the globe from Jerusalem—ten time zones away—in Portland, Oregon. And yet, Israel was always a vivid presence in our lives. Our parents took great care to draw us close to the land of Israel, the State of Israel and our family in Israel.

My father, Joshua, was born in Jerusalem. Both his mother and his father had deep roots in the land. My father's father, Eliyahu David Stampfer, was the grandson of Yehoshua Stampfer, one of the founders of Petaḥ Tikva. My great-great grandfather made his way mostly on foot from his native Hungary to Eretz Yisrael. My father's mother, Nechama Frank, for whom I'm named, was a daughter of Rabbi Zvi Pesach Frank, who for decades served as Ashkenazic chief rabbi of Jerusalem.

In 1947, my father and mother went to study for the year in Jerusalem. My father was in his third year of rabbinical school at the Jewish Theological Seminary; it was my mother's first visit to Eretz Yisrael. They lived in the home of my great grandfather, Rabbi Frank, on Malachi Street and took classes at the Hebrew University on Mt. Scopus. With the United Nation's vote for partition of Palestine their studies virtually came to an end and they focused their energies on their work in the Haganah. By the springtime of that year my mother was expecting their first child. The family urged my parents to return to America. It was one thing to keep them safe, but adding an infant would increase the strain on everyone. Reluctantly they returned to the United States and my brother, Shaul Yechiam, was born in June, 1948, in Atlanta.

My father had 15 aunts and uncles and numerous first cousins in Israel, and at one point or another I met most of them. Our family spent three separate years in Israel, when my father took sabbaticals from his rabbinic obligations at Congregation Neveh Shalom.

My earliest clear three year old memory was from our 1960 voyage on the Zim Line from New York to Israel, (although I have no memory of the cross country train trip from Portland to New York). That year we lived in a small apartment in an alleyway off of Mamilla (now Agron Street) in Jerusalem, a short distance from the Jordanian border.

We returned in 1966, this time by air to London, and then after buying a car in Paris we spent a few weeks driving through Europe and finally taking a ship from Naples to Haifa. That year we lived in Nayot, in a lovely garden apartment near the Valley of the Cross in Jerusalem. When war loomed that May my parents decided to stay and so it was that I was at school, in Beit Sefer Maaleh (just blocks away from the border) when the Six Day War broke out.

Our last sabbatical was in 1973, when we arrived a month after the end of the Yom Kippur War. That year we lived in Neveh Granot, near the Israel Museum. I spent my gap year taking courses and traveling in Israel.

In addition to our trips to Israel, our Israeli relatives sometimes came to Portland. Most significant were the extended visits of two of Dad's younger cousins: Yonatan Kaplan and Gitti Frank.

Gitti's parents, Dod Avram (his name is Avraham, but he was always Dod Avram to us), and Dodah Malkah were about my parent's ages; my grandmother was one of the older children in the family—her brother Avraham one of the youngest. Dod Avram's zest for life made a clear impression on me. He loved singing songs and telling stories.

When his memoir arrived in my mailbox a few years ago I grabbed my Hebrew dictionary and immersed myself in Dod Avram's stories. I quickly realized that I wanted to translate it into English so my children and American nieces and nephews could understand it. The project took longer than I hoped, but the translation is now complete, along with historical and personal footnotes.

Certain themes weave their way through these memoirs. It is a story of roots and growth—Avraham Frank mentions many people, often with a story or reference to their background and accomplishments. It is a story of resilience, ingenuity, courage and determination. When I think of Dod Avraham I can feel the energy of his presence, his joie de vivre, his wonderful voice telling a story or singing a song. In his memoirs he is generous in his praise of others and displays a sense of wonder at the extraordinary changes he has seen in his lifetime. Over and over the themes of love of family, *yiddishkeit* and Israel thread their way throughout this book. The love and respect with which he talks about his mother and father are unmistakable and make them alive to me.

THIS WAS A LABOR OF LOVE, MY FIRST ATTEMPT AT A major translation project with all of the daunting challenge such an undertaking includes. I have tried to maintain my uncle's voice—an interesting combination of informal style along with a rich traditional vocabulary. This is his story, a collection of anecdotes and family history, as well as the history of modern Israel. Through the footnotes I have attempted to fill in some information of historical interest as well as my own memories and impressions. In the course of this research I have learned a great deal about personalities and events of which I was previously unaware. The stories and details in the footnotes supplement and enlarge the story. I invite other family members to add to these notes with their own comments, which will only enrich the descriptions in this book.

I am grateful to many people who have helped me in this endeavor. I want to thank Dr. Eliot Lefkovitz, my teacher and advisor at Spertus College, and Dr. Dean Bell, the dean of the school for allowing me to produce this work in partial fulfillment of an academic degree. I also thank Marlene Gitelman, who gave me guidance regarding transliteration; Prof. Marc Bernstein and Prof. Gershon Bacon for suggesting academic resources. I want to especially thank my brother, Shaul, for helping me understand mysterious acronyms and historical allusions (not to mention intricacies of family history). And, most importantly, I want to thank my beloved husband, Rod, whose mastery of language—both Hebrew and English—helped me in the many moments when I struggled. His patient assistance was instrumental to completing this project. I am blessed.

Everyone who reads this book owes a huge debt of gratitude to Gitti and Dani Yardeni who managed to convince Dod Avram to compose this memoir and then made it available to us all.

It is my great hope that the next generation will get a taste of what it was like to be close to those who touched and shaped history. Living at time when the State of Israel is a given fact it is easy to take for granted the miracle of its existence.

Nehama Stampfer Glogower
Ann Arbor, Michigan
December, 2011

July, 2022

As this is being prepared to press (after so many years), I have added translations for the tributes included in the original book.

The reader will probably find inconsistencies in transliteration and errors in translation, and I freely accept responsibility for these flaws and only hope they are not too egregious.

Since the initial translation I have been blessed that my dear son-in-law Joshua Boystun has joined the family. He, along with my daughter Abby, are gifted editors and provided much guidance. I am very grateful to Elizabeth Landes for her careful and helpful copyediting. Again, my thanks to my husband, Rod, without whom there would have been many more flaws to apologize for!

Questions? Comments?
Please contact Nehama Stampfer Glogower,
nglogower@gmail.com

Foreword

On the wall of my father-in-law, Avraham's spring factory, right behind the reception desk, hangs a picture in a modest frame: Against a blue background of an ocean floats a wooden tray bearing a loaf of bread. The choice of this particular image aligns with Avraham's faith in the words of Ecclesiastes, that ancient sage, regarding the characteristics a person should seek: "Cast your bread upon the water, for in the fullness of time you will find it again." (Ecclesiastes, 11:1).

Now at an advanced age, it appears that Avraham has achieved and fulfilled this verse. Beloved and honored by his family, and by those who surround him, healthy in spirit and happy with his lot in life, alert and curious as ever.

Avraham's father—the most dominant person in his life—did not expect him to be a scholar; it also seems to me that he himself never aspired to such a status in the standard meaning of the term. Despite the great respect that he bears towards Torah scholars, and his recollections attest to that, even at a young age, Avraham's turned to a life of practical pursuits. I suspect that this was prompted by his desire to be his own man, not dependent on others. Coming from a home which lacked financial resources, Avraham was prepared to pay the price of decades of backbreaking labor, both physical and emotional. Even so, I have not seen the slightest evidence that he sought riches for their own sake and much of what he accumulated, he gave away.

Rabbi Shabbetai Rosenthal, Rav Frank's secretary, told me that Reb Aryeh Levin, who was Rav Frank's brother-in-law (their wives being sisters) as well as a close personal friend, surprised him once by saying that he wished he could have Avraham's share in the world to come. This is great praise coming from a man (Reb Aryeh) who completely devoted himself to helping other with acts of loving kindness. Reb Aryeh Levin told Rav Frank about an elderly aunt of their wives who lived in Jerusalem, who was supported financially by her son in America. A time came when the son was no longer able to continue supporting his mother, and the old woman was left destitute. Avraham took his place and secretly supported her for years until her death and she never knew that the support did not come from her son. I mention this true act of tzedakah (charity) which is so characteristic of Avraham, since Avraham himself would never tell it.

By virtue of his innate intelligence and certainly the fact that he came from, as we say, "a good home," my father-in-law has developed for himself an openness and tolerance towards people and opinions that differ from his own, as well as the ability to distinguish between the essential and trivial—which is not to say that he lacks well defined opinions of his own on every topic. One event that occurred within the family illustrates this. One of the relatives abandoned the traditional way of life and joined a secular kibbutz. When his mother became old he alone was the one who took her in with him, to the kibbutz and saw to all her needs until her dying day. At the funeral, which was held for her on the kibbutz, some of the family members complained amongst themselves about the secular life the son lived on the kibbutz. Avraham immediately castigated them: "He is the only one of you who will merit heaven, because of the great respect he showed his mother in her old age!" As the years pass, my admiration and love for Avraham only grows.

Avraham once described the deep bonds and empathic identification between husband and wife that he witnessed with his uncle Reb Aryeh Levin, who accompanied his wife to the doctor saying, "Doctor, sir, my wife's foot hurts us." I tell this sweet story because after more than 60 years of marriage the lives of Avraham and my good mother-in-law, Malka, are so intertwined one with the other that it is very difficult to distinguish between the two. Much of what he says in this book could have easily been said by either of them.

It is an honor for me and my wife Gitti, their first born daughter, to help publish this memoir. Now, as Avraham has entered the tenth decade of his life, is an appropriate time to gather his thoughts and take stock of his life. Aided by his good memory, Avraham vividly describes people he knew and events that happened, often minimizing or leaving out some of his own contributions, due to his great modesty. Therefore, I have asked a few people who know him to fill in some of the missing parts, and they gladly agreed. I thank them greatly.

Dan Yardeni
Erev Pesach 5767 — 2007

Preface

by Avraham Frank

For a long time already my family has begged me to write my memoirs. They'd joke that I remember events that happened even before I was born, and they'd say that I am a walking history book. There is truth in their words. My memories include stories of people I've never met, events that I myself did not experience, and places I never visited. Nevertheless, to the best of my knowledge, everything that I will relate in this book is true.

I WAS BORN INTO ONE OF THE MOST HIGHLY REGARDED families in Jerusalem. Abba, Rabbi Zvi Pesach Frank z"tl (may his memory be a blessing), was among the greatest rabbis in the land, and one of the most important *poskim* (rabbinic legal decisors) of his generation. The Responsa Project of Bar Ilan University—approximately 400 volumes of works by important *poskim* of every generation, from the time of the gaonim until now—also includes his work, *Har Zvi*. He served as rabbi for close to 60 years, first as a judge (*dayan*) and later as the head of the *beit din* (rabbinic court) and then as the chief rabbi of Jerusalem. An important street is named for him in the Bayit V'Gan section of the city. Imma, the *rabbanit* (rabbi's wife) Gitah-Malkah, may she rest in peace, was a "woman of valor, (אשת חיל), wise and energetic and a helpmeet in all the best meaning of the word. Perhaps because of their great modesty and because of my upbringing I have refrained from writing about them and myself until this time, thinking that they would have considered it improper.

This book would not have come into existence were it not for my son-in-law, Dan Yardeni, husband of my first-born daughter Gitah, who encouraged me to do this for a long time, arguing that it is important testimony for future generations. A few days after recovering from surgery, an auspicious time to take stock of oneself, I was persuaded and so we began the work of writing.

I wanted to give my children, and their children and grandchildren a glimpse into the Jerusalem of my youth, and Tel Aviv of my adolescence and adulthood. My generation was destined to have the honor and merit to be part of establishing a renewed Jewish state in the land of Israel; my personal experience coincided with the historical and national events of that era.

What will my grandchildren and great-grandchildren know about the patriarchs and matriarchs of our family? Or the Churvah Synagogue in the Old City of Jerusalem? Who will tell them what my uncle, Rabbi Aryeh Levin, ztz"l, the rabbi of the imprisoned members of the underground, whispered in the ear of a Lechi member shortly before he was taken to the gallows? Or where I found myself during Simchat Torah, 1937?

This book answers these and other questions. There are some events and people, however, that even today, almost 60 years after the establishment of the State, I still do not wish to reveal and I will keep their secrets safe with me.

As will become evident to the reader, I have written about my parents, may they rest in peace, with great respect and longing. Their personalities and way of living enriched my world and laid out the direction of my life. It is in their memory and for the sake of the coming generations that I put into writing the story of their lives and the story of my life.

Chapter One

These are the Generations

THE FRANK FAMILY

My father, Rabbi Zvi Pesach Frank, born in the city of Kovno, Lithuania,[1] began his studies in a *klowiz* (a small synagogue) when he was five years old. The teachers would read a chapter from the *Chumash* (the Torah) and the children would review it orally. Every day his mother, my grandmother, would give him a few *kopeks* so that he could buy something for himself. However, the child—so the congregants said—would put all of it in the *Tzedaka* (charity) box of the shul. His mother was puzzled, but the boy explained: "I want the *Kadosh Barukh Hu* (Holy One Blessed Be He) to help me succeed in my learning!" And his request was granted. Within one year a more talented instructor was asked to teach him, until, at the age of 12, the highest level teacher came to his father, my grandfather, and said to him: "I can no longer continue to accept payment from you." "Why not?" his father asked. "The boy already knows more than I do," answered the teacher. Then grandfather sent Abba to learn, first in the Slobodka[2] Yeshiva and then with Rabbi Eliezer Gordon,

---
1 Kaunas.
2 The Slobodka Yeshiva was founded in Kovno in 1881, with a special emphasis on the study of *mussar* (ethics). This was a relatively novel approach and led to

Rosh Yeshiva of Telz.[3]

My grandfather, Reb Yehudah Leib Frank, had 12 brothers and one sister. Eight of his brothers emigrated to America, as many East European Jews did in those days; he is the only one who moved to Israel. Reb Shraga Feivel Frank, one of grandfather's brothers was a well to do man who provided financial support to many scholars. Reb Feivel became ill at an early age and asked that, when the time came, my grandfather should find good bridegrooms for his daughters. My grandfather went to the Volozhin Yeshiva[4] and chose outstanding husbands. The first was the Gaon (genius) Reb Yehoshua Horowitz, who later became rabbi of Alkost, Lithuania. The second was the Gaon Reb Moshe Mordechai Epstein, who became the Rosh Yeshiva of Slobodka and then later, at my father's encouragement, made *aliyah* to Israel in 1924, moved the yeshiva to Hebron and renamed it Knesset Yisrael. The third was the Gaon Reb Issur Zalman Meltzer, who served as rabbi and rosh yeshiva in Slotsk. Later he also made *aliyah* (moving to the land of Israel) with my father's help and was named Rosh Yeshiva

---

many disputes among the students and faculty as they struggled to determine a balance between Talmud study and the study of ethics. This eventually led to a split in the yeshiva in 1897. Stampfer, Shaul. 2010. Slobodka, Yeshiva of. YIVO Encyclopedia of Jews in Eastern Europe. http://www.yivoencyclopedia.org/article.aspx/Slobodka_Yeshiva_of.

3 The Telz Yeshiva became an important institution in 1883, when Eliezer Gordon became its head. He innovated changes such as classes based on proficiency, testing and a set schedule. When Rabbi Gordon attempted to introduce mussar study to the curriculum the students resisted, claiming it took time away from their talmud studies. A student strike over this issue closed the yeshiva for a few months in 1897. Stampfer, Shaul. 2010. Telz, Yeshiva of. YIVO Encyclopedia of Jews in Eastern Europe. http://www.yivoencyclopedia.org/article.aspx/Telz_Yeshiva_of.

4 The Volozhin Yeshiva was the preeminent yeshiva in Eastern Europe for most of the 19th century. Founded in 1803 by Chayim ben Yitzchak (Chayim of Volozhin), a disciple of the Vilna Gaon, learning took place 24 hours a day, with no vacations. The yeshiva closed in 1892 in the wake of external pressures by the Russian government and internal disputes. Stampfer, Shaul. 2010. Volozhin, Yeshiva of. YIVO Encyclopedia of Jews in Eastern Europe. http://www.yivoencyclopedia.org/article.aspx/Volozhin_Yeshiva_of

at Etz Chayim in Jerusalem. The fourth was the Gaon Reb Shepsel (Shabbtai) Kremer, who lived in America and was the rabbi of Boston.

In 1887, when he was 35 years old, my grandfather became an emissary of the Jewish community of Kovno and was sent to buy land in Israel. Before he departed he summoned his son back from the Telz Yeshiva and told him something like this: "You are my first born son. You must recite the *kiddush* (blessing over wine) in the house for Shabbat and *Yom Tov* (holidays) and help your mother care for your younger brothers while I'm gone. You take care of the family until I return."

My father, born in 1872, was only about 15 years old at the time, and was already recognized as a great scholar. He followed his father's orders and returned to the *beit midrash* (study hall) of Kovno to learn with the high level students of Rabbi Isaac Elchanan Spektor. Rav Spektor was one of the leading rabbis and *poskim* in Eastern Europe. Rabbis from around the world, including England and the United States, turned to him with their questions. He served as Kovno's rabbi for over 30 years and was also a public leader whose directives were followed without question by rabbis in communities throughout Europe. He fought to protect the rights of his people and sought to bring the deplorable condition of Russian Jews to worldwide attention. Rav Spektor was an important supporter of the *Chibbat Tziyyon* movement[5] and encouraged the settlement of *Eretz Yisrael* not merely in words, but in actual deeds. So, for example, Rav Spektor forbade the use of etrogs (citrons) grown in

---

5   Ḥibbat Tziyon or Ḥovevei Zion was an organization founded in 1884 which promoted settlement of the land of Palestine, and were the primary members of the First Aliyah, when 25,000 Jews came to Palestine between 1888-1903. Gilbert, Martin, *Israel, A History*, (New York: William and Morrow Company, 1998), 5.

the Island of Corfu—which were sold throughout Europe as one of the four species used on Sukkot –in order to support the export of etrogs which were cultivated in the land of Israel. He ruled that land in Israel could be worked during the *Shemitta* (Sabbatical) year, if it had previously been sold to a gentile—in order to ease the burden of Jewish agriculture in the land. The well known Yeshiva University in New York is named after him, "The Rabbi Isaac Elhanan Yeshiva," as well as the Naḥalat Yitzchak neighborhood in Tel Aviv.[6]

Rav Yitzchak Elhanan very quickly recognized Abba's sharp mind and diligence. He was quite fond of my father, became close to him and would often converse with him on topics of Torah. On Shabbat the Rav would invite my young father to stroll with him alongside the Neman (Nemunos) River, on whose banks the city of Kovno was built. Those walks reduced the desecration of the Shabbat, for when the Jews saw the rabbi strolling by the river they would greet him and, at least in his presence, they would refrain from renting sail boats for river excursions.

Grandfather, Reb Yehudah Leib Frank, embarked on his journey. He went first to Odessa, a city on the Black Sea, and from there he sailed to *Eretz Yisrael*.[7] Along the way the ship anchored in Salonika,[8] Greece in order to take on

---

[6] Rabbi Spektor, 1817-1896 was highly regarded by traditional Jews throughout the world, as well as by the Russian authorities, who viewed him as the representative of traditional Russian Jewry. He was considered to be moderate in his halakhic rulings and worked at maintaining relations with the growing secular Jewish groups. Salmon, Yosef. 2010. Spektor, Yitsḥak Elḥanan. YIVO Encyclopedia of Jews in Eastern Europe. http://www.yivoencyclopedia.org/article.aspx/Spektor_Yitshak_Elhanan

[7] I have chosen to retain the designation *Eretz Yisrael* instead of Palestine.

[8] (Thessaloniki) was a port located in north-east Greece. The Jewish community there dates back to before the Common Era. In 1900, the Jewish population was about 80,000 out of a total population of 173,000. The Jewish community was very active in commerce, banking and trade. They also controlled the port. By the beginning of World War II, the Jewish population was 56,000. Only 2,000 survived Nazi occupation. http://www.jewishvirtuallibrary.org/jsource/judaica/ejud_0002_0017_0_17360.html

food and water. It was Friday, shortly before the beginning of *Shabbat*. The passengers were surprised to learn that the ship would not be able to sail until Sunday, since most of the waterfront workers were Jews, and the Port of Salonika was closed on *Shabbat*. On Sunday, the workers returned and the ship continued on its way to Israel. When it reached the shores of Jaffa—for it couldn't really be called a port—the ship anchored at sea and then Arab stevedores appeared in small wooden boats.[9] After the passengers boarded the boats the stevedores threw luggage from one to another and rowed the passengers to the shore.

My grandfather traveled for a year and a half in Israel. He went to Jerusalem, Rishon Letziyyon,[10] Zichron Yaacov,[11] and visited other towns and settlements until he found a parcel of land for sale in the Sharon Valley, where the town of Hadera[12] now stands. Unfortunately, the sheik who owned the property lived in Beirut and grandfather had to wait several months until the sheik arrived. Only then was he able to successfully close the deal, buy the land and return to Kovno.

9 Jaffa lacked a true port, so ships were unable to dock there. The author Shai Agnon, described the arrival of a young pioneer in Jaffa: "Two or three men came over to him [aboard ship]. One grabbed his knapsack, the other took his suitcase, and the third one pulled him along ... and he found himself sitting on a small boat bobbing between rocks and boulders ... salt water splashed on his face and hands and bit into his eyes ... The boatsmen leaned on their oars to overcome the turbulent sea, all the while cursing and yelling at one another ... the boat continued until Yitzchak wondered if he would ever arrive when suddenly a boatman yanked him up and put him on dry land." *Tmol Shilshom* (Only Yesterday), (Jerusalem: Shocken, 1946), 39. (Heb.)
10 Rishon Leẓiyon was the first village to be built by Jewish settlers from outside Palestine, in 1882. Baron Edmond de Rothschild established the Carmel Oriental wine cellars there. Gilbert, p.6
11 Established in 1882 was founded by Jewish immigrants from Romania. Funded by Baron Edmond de Rothschild, it is named in memory of his father. Gilbert, p.6
12 "Russian Jews, members of the Lovers of Zion who had emigrated from Vilna, Riga and Kovno founded their own village in 1890. They called it by the Arabic name, Ḥadera (The Green), after the emerald green colour of the swamp vegetation around them. They could not have chosen a less hospitable site. It was not only local Arabs who tormented them, but the malarial mosquito. More than half of the inhabitants of Ḥadera died of malaria in the first twenty years of its existence." Gilbert p.9

When my grandfather informed Reb Yitzḥak Elhanan Spektor that he intended to move to Israel together with his family, the Rav told him: "Go to *Eretz Yisrael*, but your son must continue his Torah learning there. I see in him the future of the nation." Grandfather followed his instructions and sent his first born son to learn in Jerusalem even before the rest of the family moved.

In 1888, just about 16 years old, my father set out on his way, after loving embraces and kisses from his parents and siblings. His cousin, Rav Shmuel Shenkar traveled with him. When they arrived in Jaffa a problem arose: they were missing the necessary documents, and the Turkish customs officials did not allow them to disembark. With no alternative, the two remained on deck and sailed on to Alexandria, Egypt. In Alexandria, as Jews did in those days, they turned to the synagogue and joined the prayer services there.[13] The *gabbai* (synagogue official) spoke with the two and realized that two scholars were standing before him. He called out to the congregation, "We must help these young people get to *Eretz Yisrael*." The venerable community of Alexandria pulled together to help and were able to arrange the documents. One week later, when the ship returned to Jaffa, my father and his cousin were aboard and this time they were permitted to reach land.

In Jaffa my father met Reb Moshe Todrosovitz (the father of David Tidhar, who was one of the first Jewish officers in the Mandate's police, and afterwards the first Jewish private detective in Israel, and editor of the *Encyclopedia of*

---

13 The Jewish community in Alexandria, Egypt dated back to 332 BCE, Alexander the Great himself encouraged Jews to move there. Until the 1940's a large Jewish population still lived there—close to 80,000. After the establishment of the State of Israel and subsequent wars between Israel and Egypt, the vast majority of the Jewish population left. Today there are fewer than 50 Jews in Alexandria. http://www.ou.org/index.php/jewish_action/article/71201/When my grandmother traveled to the United States in 1925 with my father and uncle they took the train to Alexandria and sailed from there.

the Founders and Builders of Israel). Reb Moshe's fame had preceded him as someone who would help any Jew who arrived in the land. He would invite the new arrivals to eat in his home and assist them during their first steps in the unfamiliar land. He hosted Abba in his home and helped the young scholar on his way to Jerusalem.[14]

Armed with a warm recommendation from Rav Yitzchak Elhanan Spektor, father was accepted at the Etz Chayim Yeshiva, the largest and most important yeshiva in Jerusalem in those days. Rav Shmuel Salant,[15] Jerusalem's rabbi at the time, was an undisputed authority for the Ashkenazic Jewish community of Jerusalem as a rabbi and *posek*, and as community leader for every matter. He was never formally chosen to lead and he used to say, "No one can remove me from office, since no one ever appointed me to it!" There are many wonderful stories told about him and I've chosen one to include here:

Two great scholars of that generation, the rabbi of Kalish, Reb Meir Auerbach (whom I will mention later on) and Rav Yehoshua Mekutna lived and learned together in Jerusalem. Every time they had a difference of opinion they would come to Rav Shmuel Salant to decide who was correct, and every time he ruled in accordance with Rav Yehoshua Mekutna. One time Reb Meir Auerbach got angry and suggested that the next time they come to Rav Shmuel Salant

---

14 Todrosovitz came to Israel in 1891 from the town of Projani, near Brisk, Lithuania. His wife was hesitant to leave their home. Their children had all died in infancy, but Moshe Betzalel assured her that by the merit of living in the land they would have children who reached adulthood, Sure enough, after losing another daughter, their son, David, was born in 1897 Moshe Betzalel became a businessman and leader in Jaffa, and was known for his hospitality and aid to those who made aliya. He died in 1927, and his wife, Esther Rachel, died in 1946. Tidhar, David, *Encyclopedia of the Founders and Builders of Israel*, 413. tidhar.tourolib.org

15 Rav Salant was born in Bialystok in 1816. His brilliance was recognized at an early age and he was ordained when he was bar mitzvah. He took his name from the town of Salant, where he made his home. He made *aliyah* in 1841. Tidhar, 284-85.

they would trade– Rav Yehoshua Mekutna would present the opinion of Reb Meir Auerbach and Reb Meir Auerbach would present the opinion of Rav Yehoshua Mekutna. "And we'll see," said Reb Meir Auerbach, "how the rabbi will rule." When they presented their arguments to Rav Shmuel Salant, Reb Shmuel was shocked and asked, "Reb Yehoshua! What happened to you this time?"

RAV SHMUEL, REALIZING THAT HE WAS DEALING WITH A brilliant and dedicated student who learned with both day and night, became close with Abba and arranged for him to learn in *chavruta* (partnership) with a young man who had recently become engaged to his granddaughter. The young man, Reb Yechiel Michel Tukochinski (who, in time, became the head of the Etz Chayim Yeshiva and was the creator of an astronomical calendar of Jewish holidays) came one day to Rav Shmuel Salant and complained, "I can no longer continue to learn with Zvi Pesach." "Why not?" the rabbi asked. "We've learned the tractate *Yevamot* already 40 times and now he wants to review it again!" The rav called my father and asked for an explanation. "Now that I finally understand the tractate well, I want to go back and simply enjoy the sweetness of the *gemara*, Talmud (text)" Abba answered him.

SOME MONTHS AFTER MY FATHER ARRIVED IN ISRAEL, my grandfather, Reb Yehudah Leib Frank arrived, along with my grandmother Malkah, neé Shulman, and their son, Tanchum. One daughter, Tzippy had married and emigrated to America. A second daughter, Yenta, married Rav Avraham Yaakov Orlinski and lived in Zichron Yaakov. Their son, Ze'ev Velvel learned in yeshiva in Jerusalem. And their youngest daughter, Pesha, married Yitzchak Gavrilovich and they too went to the United States.

My grandfather, my grandmother and their son Tanchum were among the founders of the settlement of Hadera, whose residents were primarily from Vilna, Kovno, and Riga. They lived in an abandoned Arab *khan* (inn) built on a hill surrounded on all sides by swampland. The pioneers of Hadera suffered greatly from malaria that came from the swamps, from lack of experience in agricultural work, and the machinations of the Turkish government and local Bedouin tribes. My grandparents also suffered from malaria and had to leave the area along with the rest of the settlers. After the plague was overcome, a number of settlers returned to Hadera, but my grandparents moved to Jerusalem. My grandfather died in 1913 and my grandmother lived alone in the city. Their son Tanchum stayed in Hadera as a farmer and lived out his life there. Many of his descendants continued to live there and, as is well known, since then it has become a large and important city in Israel.

My oldest brother, who was also named Tanchum, told me that in 1909, when he was about 10 years old, he went with our grandparents to visit their son in Hadera. Along the way they were attacked by bandits who demanded gold and jewelry. Discussion and a parley began, and the Arab wagon driver protected his passengers, telling the bandits, "These are just poor old people—even were you to kill them you wouldn't find anything." In the meantime, the residents of Hadera saw that grandfather and grandmother were delayed and sent four riders to meet them. When the bandits saw the approaching riders they were taken aback and fled without injuring the passengers or their possessions.

In 1946, when I lived in Petach Tikva, I met an old Jewish man, one of the elders of the city, whose name was Baruch Dinovitz (the son of Reb Mordechai Dinovitz, one of the first "Bialystokers" who settled in Petach Tikva[16]). When Baruch heard that I was a grandson of Reb Yehudah Leib Frank, he squeezed my hands warmly and said: "I once met your grandfather." I was surprised, because my grandfather lived in Hadera, not Petach Tikva. But Baruch Dinovitz told me that many years ago, in the early morning while he was plowing his field, he saw a Jewish man waving a white handkerchief. He halted his mules and approached the man and asked his name. It turned out that he had been traveling from Jerusalem to Hadera and the wagon broke down. Baruch took him to the *shul* (synagogue) in Petach Tikva and then invited him home for a meal. It turned out that my grandfather was about to arrange an engagement for his son Tanchum to a young woman from Petach Tikva, Hinke Lipkis. And so the meeting with my grandfather was etched in Baruch Dinovitz's memory.

In those early days of the previous century my grandfather went to America to participate in a nephew's wedding. He discovered that the family had greatly increased, and there he met about 300 people who were all descendants of the Frank family of Kovno. Grandfather stayed in the United States for some time and took the opportunity of becoming an American citizen, even though he had no

---

16 Dinowitz was a successful scribe and book dealer in Bialystok, Russia. In 1882 he helped purchase land in Petach Tikva with an eye towards making *aliyah*. His wife, Sara Gutta, and three children moved to *Eretz Yisrael* soon thereafter, living in the village of Yehudiah and working the land in Petach Tikva, until such time that it would be safe to live in Petach Tikva. Mordechai Dinovitz remained in Bialystok conducting his business, which included importing etrogim (citrons) from Israel. When Mordechai heard about the difficult conditions facing his family he asked his wife to return. She refused, insisting that the children be raised in the land of Israel. In 1885 he wound up his business and joined his family in Petach Tikva. Tidhar p.425

intention of settling there.[17] On his way back to Israel he visited several Jewish communities in Europe and stayed with his cousin in Warsaw, who was married to Dr. Popko, who directed a hospital there.

Decades later I injured my finger and went to the Kupat Cholim clinic on Zamenhoff Street in Tel Aviv. I waited to see Dr. Lazer Popko, when, to my surprise, the nurse came out asking, "Who is the Frank fellow?" I identified myself and she called me back to see the doctor immediately. I didn't recognize him, but he asked, "Are you the grandson of Reb Yehudah Leib Frank?" "Yes," I answered, and he told me about my grandfather's visit in Warsaw in 1907. "Your grandfather stayed with us on his way from America to Israel and celebrated *Pesach* (Passover) with us. My parents were quite excited at his arrival and the *Pesach Seder* (the ritual meal the first night of Passover) in his company was the most beautiful one that I remember from my youth.

THE SHAPIRO FAMILY

My mother, Gitah Malkah, was the granddaughter of Rabbi Chaim Yaakov Shapiro, a modest, humble and irreproachable scholar. He served on the *Beit Din* of Rabbi Yitzchak Elhanan Spektor in Kovno for 20 years, and was then invited by Rabbi Shmuel Salant to serve as the head of the *Beit Din* of Jerusalem.

Rabbi Chaim Yaakov Shapiro was born in Kovno, Lithuania, and lost his father Menachem, when he was only five

---

17 The current law requires that the parent who is an American citizen can transmit U.S. citizenship to his/her child as long as the parent has met certain residency requirements. In certain cases grandparents can pass citizenship along to grandchildren younger than 18. Until the mid-1920's, however, there was no residency requirement, and the citizenship could be handed down. So even though my father, and both of his parents were born in Eretz Yisrael, they were all U.S. citizens. When the law changed they had to come live in the United States or give up their U.S. citizenship. Interestingly enough, my father had U.S. citizenship from the Frank side of the family as well as on the Stampfer side.

years old. He grew up in the home of his grandfather, Rabbi Leibele Kovner, a judge and *posek* who had a remarkable memory. Rabbi Leibele Kovner kept only the Babylonian Talmud in his home. He would peruse books and pass them along to others. He only needed to read a book once for him to remember its contents.

When Rabbi Chaim Yaakov was of age, his grandfather matched him with Esther Libah of Ruznyo, Lithuania. After the wedding the young couple decided to move to *Eretz Yisrael*. They packed their belongings, bade farewell to the family and headed south towards Odessa. While they were en route a messenger from Rabbi Leibel Kovner intercepted them, pleading that they return to Kovno. Rabbi Yaakov Shapiro was unable to refuse his grandfather's request. The couple turned on their heels and went back to Kovno. Rabbi Leibele Kovner passed away in 1853 and was buried in the city's Jewish cemetery. Fifty years later the cemetery was moved and when the members of the *chevra kaddisha* (burial society) exhumed the body they were amazed to discover that it was intact and well preserved. This fact was recorded in the community history books as a strange and unique phenomenon, as if it were a wonder or a miracle.[18]

After his death, his grandson, Rabbi Chaim Yaakov Shapiro was named to replace him on the *beit din*. Thus a strong collegial and personal relationship grew between him and the great *posek*, Rabbi Yitzchak Elhanan Spektor.

---

18 A similar story is told of my grandmother and namesake, Nechama Frank Stampfer, who died and was buried in Akron, Ohio in 1939. This "temporary" burial lasted some 40 years, until her body was exhumed and reburied next to her mother's grave on the Mount of Olives. When Rabbi Frank died in 1961 there was no Jewish access to the Mount of Olives cemetery, so that plot was available in 1978. When my grandmother's coffin was opened (necessary because in Israel bodies are wrapped and placed directly in the ground) her body was intact.

Around 1879 Rabbi Chaim Yaakov Shapiro and his wife Esther Libah were able to fulfill their dream, and they made *aliyah*. I've personally seen the accounts book of the Churvat Rabbi Yehudah HeChassid [synagogue] and saw a permit from Rabbi Shapiro, dated 1880 for plastering and painting work in the synagogue. That's how I was able to determine that his *aliyah* took place before then.

While still in Kovno, their son, David, lost his wife at an early age and he was left with five orphan children. In order to ease his son's burden, or, perhaps so that she could help him along the journey to Israel, my grandfather suggested that his granddaughter, Gitah Malkah, should accompany him to Israel and that he would raise her. That's how my mother came to Jerusalem.

Ruzhany, Esther Libah's birthplace was infamous for a blood libel accusation that took place in 1659 right before Passover, when the body of a Christian child was found in the cellar of a Jewish home. As would periodically happen in those days the Jews were accused of using the blood of Christian children in order to prepare *matza* (unleavened bread used on Passover). Many Jews were incarcerated and tortured; since there was no physical evidence, the court condemned the entire community to death. Two Jewish leaders decided to accept the blame upon themselves in order to spare the rest. The court offered clemency in exchange for their repudiation [of their Jewish faith and agree to convert to Christianity], but the accused sharply rejected the offer and remained imprisoned until the sentence was carried out. The agitated community sent an emissary to the king and succeeded in convincing him that this was blood libel. The king granted a pardon for the accused, but tragically the emissary's return was delayed.

When he finally arrived in Ruzhany, it turned out that the two righteous men had been executed the previous day.[19]

Their descendants added the name "Zackheim" to their names, an acronym for *zera kodesh hem*, that is to say, the descendents of the holy ones who gave their lives for *Kiddush Hashem* (the sanctification of God's name). My mother's grandmother, Esther Libah, was from the Zackheim family, an offspring of those courageous Jews who refused to renounce their religion even though it cost them their lives.

My Parent's Marriage

When my mother became of age, her grandfather, Rabbi Chaim Yaakov Shapiro, sought an appropriate match for his granddaughter. Many young scholars wanted to marry her, but grandfather had heard good things from Rabbi Shmuel Salant about his beloved student, Zvi Pesach Frank, the *gaon* from Etz Chayim and he decided that he would be a good match for his granddaughter. One evening the two of them, grandfather and Abba, davened together in shul and after *maariv* (evening prayers), the rabbi invited Abba to his home so that he could talk with him and get to know him. While they were conversing, evening fell, and from one of the rooms a thin attractive young woman emerged, lit the lantern wicks, quickly moving from one to the other, and then disappeared in the blink of an eye. That was the first time Abba saw Imma and he indicated his agreement to the match. The next time they met was under the *chuppah* (wedding canopy) in 1894. Abba was then 21, and Imma 17.

They had 14 children and here are the names in their birth order: Channah, Sarah, Tanchum, Nechama, Pesha,

---

[19] For a full account of this event, see jewishgen.org/yizkor/ruzhany/ruz010.html, which includes the text of a special selichot which was recited yearly in Ruzhany.

Rachel, Rivka, Mina, Yaakov, Zalman, Yehudah, me—Avraham, and after me, Esther and Feivel. During the time of shortages and hunger which afflicted Jerusalem during the First World War, three of their children died of illness: Sarah, Rivkele, and Zalman. It wasn't possible to save them, since the wonder drug penicillin was developed only years later. A deep grief fell upon my parents, but despite their mourning, our home continued to be an active and lively place, and full of visitors.

My parents complemented one another in their unique characteristics and held fast to one another; our home was filled with the fear of heaven, respect and love. My father continued to devote all of his time to study, and my mother, who was a wise and practical woman, was the bridge between him and the rest of the family and the community. Cooking was not her strong suit (I received full compensation for this lack when I married my wife Malkah!)[20], but she maintained our home as a warm and inviting place, providing help and assistance to all in need.

Even though Abba was an important and highly regarded man in the community, he remained modest and humble, never wanting to be a burden or to trouble others. He never asked for anything, not even for his children to bring him a glass of water or his slippers when he came in from the cold Jerusalem streets. Once the entire family was sitting down to eat and we had forgotten to prepare the small cup of olive oil he used to sip each day before the meal—which he believed aided in digestion. Abba arose

---

20 I can certainly attest to that fact. Even as a child I could recognize that Doda Malka was an outstanding cook. Dodah Esther once told me a story that her father, Rav Frank, once came home from a long day of learning and helped himself to some soup simmering on the stove. Gittah Malkah was upset because he was eating the starch she had prepared for the next day's ironing.

from his place, went to the kitchen and poured it himself. "Why didn't you ask us?" we asked, for all of us children were around the table. "I didn't want to trouble anyone," he answered simply.

When my parents got married the primary source of income for most of the city's inhabitants were the support funds that came from Jewish communities throughout the world. The Jews of the Diaspora always considered the inhabitants of the land of Israel as their emissaries who were fulfilling the *mitzvah* of living in the land. Therefore the Diaspora Jews fulfilled their own obligation by sustaining them and tending to their needs. The accepted practice for collecting the necessary funds was through the agency of the "Rabbi Meir Ba'al Haness Fund" collection boxes, which were placed in businesses and Jewish public places or by way of "rabbinic agents," designated emissaries who went to the lands of the Diaspora for this specific purpose.[21] After collection, the funds were brought to Israel and distributed among the *kollelim* (organizations that fund full time study of Talmud) that had been established according to the country of origin.[22] These funds were called *chalukah* (distribution money) and were distributed by designated *gabaim* (volunteer officials) to the inhabitants of Jerusalem according to certain criteria. In 1886 the European communities established the "Committee of Administrators and Clerks" in order to centralize and coordinate the fundraising and distribution among the various *kollelim*. But alongside the righteous and pure minded *gabbais* who

---

21 For an interesting discussion of the use of the *pushke*, collection box, see "The Pushke and its Development," in *Families, Rabbis and Education: Traditional Jewish Society in Nineteenth-Century Eastern Europe*, by Shaul Stampfer.

22 Although *kollel* usually refers to an organization that supports scholars through a yeshiva or a community, in this case it refers to committees that centrally collected and distributed funds for immigrants to Israel . Stampfer, p.116.

conducted the holy work of distribution of the *chalukah* money appropriately, there were also those who took care of their own households, and not their communities. Great bitterness developed among those who saw themselves as deprived, especially during the days of World War I, when money could not be transferred from those countries at war with Turkey, a time when many Jews in Israel came close to starvation.

Immediately following their wedding in 1894, my parents moved into the Battei Machse neighborhood near the southern wall of the Old City of Jerusalem. Approximately 100 families lived there; it was run by a tenants committee, led by the *gabbais* Reb Moshe Zaks and Yeshayahu Shlang, who strictly managed the order and sanitation of the neighborhood. [Note by Avraham Frank: *The physician, Dr. Neuman, described Battei Machse as follows: All of the apartments are full of light and air and are comfortably equipped. Each one consists of two rooms and a kitchen. The plaza on which the apartments are built are adjacent to the southern wall of the city and has a lovely view of the Mt. of Olives and its surroundings. All of the buildings face the large and spacious courtyard and are situated with such a pleasant design that these dwellers suffer from illnesses far less than the rest of the Jewish inhabitants of Jerusalem*] My family lived in Battei Machse for 36 years and it wasn't until 1930 that my parents left the neighborhood and moved to a house they built in "Keren Avraham" outside the city walls. In Battei Machse we had two rooms—one large and one small. The parents slept in the small room and we, the children, in the large one. At night we'd move the dining room table, spread mattresses on the floor, recite the *Shema* aloud and lay down to sleep, all the children lying side by side on the mattresses. Because of the limited financial circumstances, we did not heat the home in the winter, and when Imma burned coals under a pot to boil water, we would all gather around it in order to warm up a bit.

Abba—Judge and *Posek*

In 1897 Rabbi Yitzchak Elchanan Spektor, the *posek* of the generation, in whose yeshiva my father had learned, passed away in Kovno and there was great mourning throughout the Jewish world. In our city of Jerusalem, the Sephardic rabbi, the *Gaon* Rabbi Shlomo Alfendi, announced that the next day there would be a public mourning in the Rabbi Yochanan ben Zakkai Synagogue. A large crowd gathered and the synagogue was filled to capacity. For half an hour Rabbi Shlomo Alfendi eulogized Rabbi Yitzchak Elhanan Spektor. He spoke of his greatness, expertise, broad and deep knowledge, his legal decisions, his great wisdom, his wonderful attributes and meticulousness.

Abba, Rav Zvi Pesach Frank, ztz"l

When he finished his eulogy, some members of the Ashkenazi community approached him and asked, "How can this be, Rabbi Alfendi? You have never been in Kovno, and Rav Spektor, of blessed memory, didn't visit Jerusalem. How did you know all these things?"

Rav Alfendi was not at all disconcerted. He pointed at my father and answered, "By way of this young man who was his student I know how great Rav Spektor was over there," for Rabbi Alfendi knew my father well and held many long and learned discussions with him.

Abba's renown went before him. The rabbis of Jerusalem appreciated his understanding, his expertise and sharp mind. Rav Shmuel Salant received questions and problems of *halakha* (Jewish law) from communities throughout the world. He began to pass those letters along to Abba so that he could prepare answers. When he saw my father's clarity of thought and depth of analysis, he passed along even more letters. Rav Salant saw that my father was not pleased with this increasing burden. "Rav Zvi Pesach," the rabbi asked, "Why are you so reluctant?" "It interferes with my learning," he replied. "Learners I have plenty of—*posekim* I don't have enough. You will be a *posek*," Rav Salant firmly decreed.

And so, in 1902, before he was even 30 years old, my father was named a member of the great *beit din* of the Churvah Synagogue in Jerusalem. Rav Moshe Nachum Wallenstein and Rabbi Leib Dayan also served on this *beit din*. He was the youngest of the judges and before he accepted the appointment he turned to Rav Salant with a request: "This is a great responsibility. I want to learn and prepare before I take this demanding position upon myself." The rabbi agreed and my father went down to Jaffa, in quasi-exile from his home and surroundings. For six months my father sequestered himself in Jaffa. He took a room in the house of someone he had known from the day he arrived, Reb Moshe Betzalel Todrosovitz-Tidhar. There he immersed himself in the study of *Yoreh Deah* and *Orach Chayim* [23] and in the works of several *poskim*. He left his room only to *daven* (pray)—the rest of the time he learned alone.

One day Rabbi Salant heard that father had been offered a position as head of a prestigious European yeshiva. The

---

23 These are two of the four sections of the *Shulchan Aruch*, the primary code of Jewish law. The section of Orach Chayim deals with day to day mitzvot: Prayers, Shabbat, holidays and the like. The section of Yoreh Deah deals with laws regarding what is permissible and what is forbidden, such as laws of kosher food, marital laws [niddah] monetary interest, vows, mourning and so on.

rabbi quickly urged him to return to Jerusalem and begin serving as a *posek* and judge in the rabbinical *beit din*.

Abba was valiant in the court. He could quickly grasp intricate and multi-layered issues and was able to distinguish between primary and secondary points, between the grain and the chaff. In his wisdom he knew how to clarify and unravel complications, and produce a clear and practical *halachic* answer to the presenting problem. He made rulings with clarity and courage and shouldered the responsibility that is reserved only for those with the most profound expertise in *halacha*. Along with this he endured the pain of those who were suffering. He did not rest until he found a solution to the problems of the downtrodden and particularly to the sufferings of *agunot* (women anchored in a marriage unable to obtain a divorce or be declared a widow), of which there were more than a few in Jerusalem following the First World War.

Abba was never tardy for court deliberations and never showed contempt for the litigant's time, as was often customary then—and, regretfully, also today. My oldest brother, Tanchum, served as a secretary in the chief rabbinate in Jerusalem for 42 years, and witnessed father's tremendous discipline, beginning each deliberation at the specified time, and respecting the litigants. Abba would say, "The people's time is precious." After Abba died Tanchum saw how judges would ignore other people's timetables, scheduling a deliberation for a certain hour and showing up late, smug and relaxed. "Had Abba been alive, he would have fired them on the spot and not permit such contempt," Tanchum told me. It wasn't long before Abba was chosen to be a head of the *Beit Din* and served for decades as the head of the *Beit Din*, as chief rabbi of Jerusalem and a member of the committee of the chief rabbinate.

Abba's personality and judicial temperament are described in the book, *Conversations With the Supreme Court Judge Ḥaim Cohen*,[24] written by Michael Sasser. This is what Justice Cohen said:

"I loved him very much, I actually revered him ... Rav Frank was a warm man, and full of compassion that revealed great understanding of the human souls who stood before him. You always had the impression that he also bore their suffering."

And regarding the freeing of *agunot*, Justice Cohen wrote:

"In 1959 I traveled to the Soviet Union. The day before my departure a man and woman came to me. The man said that she had been widowed and her late husband had two brothers in Riga, both of whom were married to non-Jews. He added that Rav Frank had said that if he received testimony to this fact, he would free her from the obligation of *yibbum* (the requirement of levirate marriage). The judges here told me, 'Go to a *beit din* there and bring the brothers to the *beit din* so they can testify.' I arrived in Riga *erev* Yom Kippur. I was in the city only for Yom Kippur and already the following day I had to leave. I knew that I could do a great *mitzvah*. I found the address of the two brothers and went to them. Of course there was no *beit din* there, and all I could bring back was what they told me, that they were

---

24 Chayim Cohen, supreme court justice and winner of the Israel Prize was one of the giants of justice in the State of Israel. He had a unique career: attorney, a founder of the judicial system in Israel, the first state prosecutor, minister of justice for a short time, government legal advisor for the State of Israel in the 1950's, president of the committee for civil rights. Sasser's book was published in 1990 by Keter Publishing, Jerusalem (pp. 204-207) Although he came from a religious family and spent time in yeshiva, he gave up his religious faith, saying "Judaism requires man to love God. But how can you love God when every day and hour He is cruel to you." A champion of human rights, he died in 2002 at the age of 91. http://www.haaretz.com/news/justice-haim-cohen-founding-father-of-legal-system-dies-at-91-1.48102.

married to non-Jews. I came to his [Rav Frank's] home on Malachi Street—this was just a few months before his death. I told the story and the judges who were sitting with him began to examine me. And he—I remember it as if it were today—stopped me with his hands, because anything I could add would only detract. And he actually released her based on this brief testimony. However, only a very few rabbis would have this type of fortitude.

"It wasn't that he had great courage, nor was it the boldness to create great reforms or deviate from the *Halacha*. He simply identified with people's suffering. He had a pure soul. He was one of the 36 righteous, if they truly exist." (from the book *Chaim Cohen—High Judge*).

Regarding the judges and rabbinical courts, Justice Cohen addressed the question: "Can we generalize and say that the Sephardic rabbis were more open and liberal, or were they more pragmatic than the Ashkenazic rabbis?"

"I never had such an impression. In the court of Rav Frank that was certainly not the case."

Regarding the question of whether rabbis today had less expertise in the law than rabbis of a generation or two earlier, he said:

"No. Even then there were rabbis of greater and lesser expertise, and it would be impossible to compare between some of them and others. This is natural and that's how it is with judges. When you appeared before a man like Rav Zvi Pesach Frank you knew that you were in the presence of an outstanding personality. This is not a judge you would run into on an ordinary day. But the problem is not in the status of the judges, rather in their approach towards making judgments. Today you find that the rabbis who succeeded in making personal status laws hateful—and in its wake, religion in general—to the great majority of the Israeli public. I had intended and prayed, as did Ben Gurion (the first prime minister of Israel), that the rabbinical courts to be established would have the wisdom to make the Jewish religion beloved to the general community—all the more so because there is so much beauty in it."

Years later Supreme Court Justice Chaim Cohen wrote an autobiography and in it he mentioned Abba: "He was a purely righteous man in all the meanings of those two words. He was more compassionate, merciful, patient and kind than any other judge or *dayan* that I have encountered in my entire professional life." (Cohen, Chayim, A Personal Introduction—Autobiography. Dvir publishing, 2005)

A significant portion of Abba's work as a *posek* did not take place within the framework of the *beit din*, but, rather, in answering the questions of Jews who came to the house to consult with him. And they came from every walk of life within the community: rabbis, emissaries, religious leaders, public servants and also the downtrodden and the poor. There were fateful deliberations that took place in the large room, dealing with problems of communal welfare—and then there were the most intimate difficulties between husband and wife, when father would use his private room. The door to our home was open to everyone and Abba treated each person respectfully, with patience and love.

I remember once such day, when a poor woman came to our house. In her hand was a slaughtered chicken and in her mouth a question: "Is this chicken kosher?" Abba examined the chicken, saw what he saw and took it into the kitchen. "Do we have a chicken in the house?" he asked Imma quietly. Without saying a word, Imma switched the chickens. Abba gave the woman our chicken and said to her, "This chicken is kosher to the highest standard." And so, without noticing the switch, the woman went on her way.

From morning until night Jews would come to ask questions and consult. Occasionally, when Abba was occupied, they would turn to Imma and, if it was something regarding inter-personal relations, she would listen carefully and sometimes protected Abba's limited time by solving the problem and finding a solution that satisfied both parties.

One Shabbat a distraught woman came to our house. "Is it permissible to accept a *get* (bill of divorce) on Shabbat?" she asked Abba. He invited her in to sit with the family, listened to her distress, and explained to her that on Shabbat he was not a *posek*. Somehow he managed to calm her and promised that he would take care of her concerns the next day. After she left Abba explained to us that this had not been the first time this woman had approached him and she always had the same request. She had been a widow who had remarried. It became clear that her husband wished to be rid of her and from time to time he would himself appear as if he were dying. He would stop breathing and become as white as plaster. The woman would become frantic, for if he'd die and leave her widowed a second time her chances for remarriage would be greatly reduced, since she would be considered a source of bad luck. And should it happen a third time, she'd be unable to wed, for then she would be a *katlanit* (a destroyer).[25]

The next day, as Abba predicted, the husband arrived in blooming health, happy and cheerful, and arranged the *get*. About two years later, in 1937, when I was in the Haganah, a few friends of mine and I arrived at an apartment on the edges of Meah Shearim in Jerusalem, where a Jew lay dead.

---

25 The talmud discusses the situation of whether it is safe for a man to marry a woman who had been widowed twice or three times, especially if the husbands had not been old or engaged in a dangerous profession.

We came there and found a Jewish man who had taken his own life by drinking poison in the bathroom. I looked at his grieving wife and couldn't believe my eyes. It was this Jerusalemite woman who had feared becoming a *katlanit*.

DURING HIS "EXILE" IN JAFFA, FATHER INTRODUCED himself to Rav Avraham Yitzchak HaCohen Kook, who, at that time, had been appointed chief rabbi of Jaffa. Rav Kook strongly sympathized with the Zionist movement and thus aroused the fierce opposition of the established *Charedi* (strictly religious) community in Jerusalem. In 1914 Rav Kook went to a rabbinical conference in Switzerland and, with the outbreak of the First World War, he was unable to return to the land of Israel. He found a temporary position as a rabbi in London, and lived there until 1919. In London he supported the political Zionists and came out sharply against those who tried to prevent the issuing of the Balfour Declaration. As you may recall, in 1917 the Balfour Declaration was issued wherein the British government announced its support of the establishment of a Jewish state in the land of Israel.

In 1919, after the end of the war, Rav Kook returned to Israel. During this period Abba already was working hard to establish a chief rabbinate for the entire land of Israel and supported the appointment of Rav Kook as its head. Members of the *Agudas Yisroel* (an organization of religious Jews opposed to political Zionism) attempted to torpedo this process and claimed that since he was a judge, my father had no right to dabble in political action such as establishing a chief rabbinate in Israel.

One Shabbat Rav Kook was invited to Jerusalem and delivered a sermon before the congregation at the Churvah

Synagogue in the Old City. That same Shabbat a *brit milah* (circumcision) was held in the synagogue for the son of Dr. Newman, one of the doctors in the Wallach Hospital and Rav Kook was invited to be the *sandek* (the one who holds the baby during the circumcision).[26] After the *kiddush* some of the *Agudas Yisroel* members, led by Rabbi Chaim Zonnenfeld and Rabbi Leib Rubin, spoke with Rav Kook and made him a tempting offer: "We want to establish a high *beit din* in Jerusalem, which you will lead."[27]

"I'll consult tomorrow with Rav Frank and I'll let you know my decision," answered Rav Kook. He came to my father and admitted that the position offered by these *Agudas Yisroel* leaders appealed to him. However my father who, as I mentioned, was pushing to appoint Rav Kook as the chief rabbi for the entire land of Israel warned him: "If you go with *Agudas Yisroel* you will neither be a rabbi nor a majority [a play on words in Hebrew—לא תהיה רב ולא תהיה רוב]." In one brief and concise statement Abba pointed out to Rav Kook that when there would be differences of opinion within the court, he would be only one among three judges; the other two *Agudas Yisroel* judges would always ally themselves against him and thus deny him the necessary majority to issue a judgment. And so, at father's counsel, and despite the continuing attempts of *Agudas Yisroel* to scuttle the plan, Rav Kook became the rabbi of Jerusalem and, with the establishment of the chief rabbinate in 1921,

---

26 Rav Kook was also the *sandek* at my father's *brit milah*..
27 *Agudas Yisroel* is a political party founded in Poland in 1912 to represent traditional conservative Jewish interests, especially in response to the Reform and Zionist movements. Although they were strongly opposed to secular Zionism, they did encourage immigration to Israel. Bacon, Gershon. 2010. Agudas Yisroel. YIVO Encyclopedia of Jews in Eastern Europe. http://www.yivoencyclopedia.org/article.aspx/AgudasYisroel. Rav Kook and Rav Frank tried to find some common ground with the secular Zionists, which set them at odds with Agudas Yisroel members.

he was chosen to be the head of the high *beit din* and thus became the first Ashkenazic chief rabbi in Israel.

Jockeying for prominence between political parties and bitter disagreements regarding appointments are not recent inventions. Even then interested parties didn't refrain from stirring the pot. One day a religious Jew came to my father and said, "Rabbi, I didn't sleep all last night because of you." My father was shaken. "Why?" "I read the slanders written about you by the *Agudas Yisroel* and *Neturei Karta*,"[28] the man answered. "So why do you read it? Throw the newspaper into the trash!" my father soothed the agitated Jew.

In 1935 my father was appointed chief rabbi of Jerusalem. His investiture in this position during such a turbulent era and time of upheaval placed him in the center of Torah life in the city.

Abba was acceptable within many circles in the city, and not only in the Ashkenazi community. A proclamation saved from the 1950's testifies to this: The Yazd [Iranian] community requested his endorsement and signature to the language of the special prayer on behalf of the soldiers of the Israel Defense Force (IDF), which still exists today.

Prayer On Behalf of the Israel Defense Force

> May the One who blessed our holy and pure ancestors, Abraham, Isaac, Jacob, Moses, Aaron, David and Solomon, bless and protect and preserve this holy congregation and all of our sons who serve in the Israel Defense Force, including those who guard the borders, who protect our land and the cities of

---

28 Literally, "Guardians of the City," this is a relatively small extremist group that actively opposes the existence of the State of Israel.

our God, from the Lebanon border to the wilderness of Egypt, from the Great Sea to the Jordan Valley, and those who serve in the air, on the sea and on land. May the Holy One Blessed Be He, in His great mercy and kindness, protect them from every trouble and injury and save them from the hand of all enemies and ambush, both internal and external—just as You defended Joshua ben Nun and his armies when they captured the land, and David ben Yishai and Yoav ben Zeruya when they fought Your wars, so may You stand beside our young men and give them the strength to totally defeat those who rise up against us. And may all of our enemies be routed before them. And raise the light of Israel in peace and spread over us Your canopy of peace. May it be Your will, Lord our God and God of our fathers, for the sake of this Torah and this moment of mercy inspire the hearts of those who stray from Your path, that they return in complete penitence and observe Your Torah, its laws and *mitzvot* as is proper, Amen.

And through the merit of observing the Torah and its *mitzvot* may we merit the complete and true redemption of Israel in the building of our holy and glorious temple speedily in our day. And say Amen.

Even during the days of the British Mandate, Abba worked towards bringing Torah centers from the Diaspora to Israel and due to his efforts many rabbis and their outstanding students came to Israel. Among them, we've already mentioned Rabbi Mordechai Epstein, the head of the Slobodka Yeshiva, who established his yeshiva in

Hebron, and Rabbi Issar Zalman Meltzer, the head of the Slotsk Yeshiva, who was appointed head of the Etz Chayim Yeshiva in Jerusalem, serving in that position until his dying day. Abba did much to draw together the hearts of the varied ideological groups that existed in Israel and didn't hesitate to deliver lenient legal decisions—within the confines of *halacha*, of course—regarding the questions they brought him, such as: the difficulties of milking [on Shabbat] on religious farms; observing *mitzvot* while on front line situations for the Palmach (an elite unit of the Haganah) or the IDF (Israel Defense Force); freeing of *agunot* and more. This was a time in Israel when many rabbis took the easy path and issued stringent decisions. The extreme sects, ultra-religious Jews never forgave him for this, but Abba never flinched, and raised the prestige of the chief rabbinate in Jerusalem, from which grew the chief rabbinate of Israel.

An incident that took place during the War of Independence: The Tehuresh Brothers used their workshop to add armor to trucks and buses used by the Jewish defense forces. They asked Abba for permission to work on Shabbat in order to protect buses that were running between Jerusalem and the besieged Gush Etzion. When he understood the situation Abba decided as follows: "Since the situation in Gush Etzion and the entire area is quite dire, and in order to save lives there is an immediate need to bring reinforcements, every delay and hindrance puts Jewish lives in danger. Therefore, I declare that it is permissible and even a commandment of *pikuach nefesh* [the requirement to break Shabbat laws in order to save a life] to work and immediately prepare armored buses, even on the holy Shabbat. *And whoever is energetic is praiseworthy.*"

My son-in-law, Dani Yardeni, told me of an incident that seemed unbelievable, given the current reality in Israeli society. It appeared in the book, *Hagar*, by Yocheved Brandes.[29] The hero of the story, Avraham Friedman, is a yeshiva student from Meah Shearim who is unable to stay on the sidelines, and joins Palmach men who lived in Kibbutz Eyn Shemer of the Shomer *ha-Tza'ir* (a rigorously secular organization). Hagar, a training officer there, noticed that the young man wasn't eating. When she asked him why, he explained that the food in the dining room was not kosher. Hagar raised this issue at the kibbutz general meeting. After a stormy discussion, which included her threat that if no solution was found all of the men in the training course would refuse to eat in the dining room, the kibbutz turned to Rabbi Zvi Pesach Frank (!) with a question of what to do. And this is what Yuchi Brandes writes in her book:

> A heavy silence reigned over the small dining room. Everyone looked at Hagar, who began to walk out with her head held high and her back upright. "One minute," called her father. He approached her, put his arm around her shoulder and turned with her towards the other members. "I suggest that we consult with the rabbi of the Haganah in Jerusalem," he said, "I have heard that the Haganah has a brilliant and open minded rabbi who advises them on questions that deal with the integration and inclusion of religious soldiers.
> The protests were particularly forceful. "To con-

---

29 Brandes was raised in an ultra-orthodox family, and later chose to be less religious, yet she remains religiously connected. http://www.haaretz.com/my-good-god-let-me-be-free-1.186579

sult with a rabbi in Jerusalem? We are almost like diaspora wretches, we're like Meah Shearim!" But when all was said and done, the majority decided that beyond the letter of the law, and without creating precedents, the members of Eyn Shemer would allow officer Hagar Ne'eman to consult with the rabbi of the Haganah in Jerusalem about food for soldier Avraham Friedman, and it goes without saying that there is no question here of a *halachic* decision, God forbid, but merely consultation and nothing more.

Hagar wrote a long and detailed letter to Rabbi Zvi Pesach Frank and described to him how difficult it would be to *kasher* [make kosher] the kibbutz kitchen in these difficult days. Two and a half weeks later a special messenger of the Haganah brought her a letter with the response. She was bursting with curiosity, but hesitated to open the envelope. Certainly he would require them to throw out the utensils and to acquire a new and double sets, she thought to herself, which would be a decision the kibbutz could not accept.

She opened the letter and warily read the short sentences:

'My respected officer, your question was difficult and important. I consulted with Rabbi Yosef Gershon Horowitz and he said to me that within the Garden of Eden there must be a bit of Hell. My message to Avraham Friedman is that he must eat warm and nutritious meals in order to fulfill the important missions that lie before him. During the time of cooking, please try not to mix meat and milk or bring non-kosher meat into the kitchen. Everything else can be as usual.

May the Holy One Blessed be He be with you, brave warriors.

Hakatan Zvi Pesach Frank
(Brandes, Yochi, *Hagar*, Published by Yediot Acharonot and Sifrei Chemed, Tel Aviv 1998, pp.205-206)

My son-in-law thought the story so hard to believe that he finally contacted the author and asked if we were dealing with literary imagination or something that really happened. It turned out that, aside from certain changes that were necessary for the story she wanted to tell, this was an event that actually took place. A yeshiva student named Avraham Havizman, who was known on the kibbutz as "the tall young man with the black hat," was killed at the age of 20 in the battle of Kastel at the entrance to Jerusalem (in her book Brandes gives him a long life), and the kibbutz was not Eyn Shemer, but rather, Gan Shmuel. The rest was complete truth.

I recall another event which took place during the siege of the Jerusalem and the shortages that came in its wake. Shmuel Eisenman, husband of Rivka, my wife Malkah's sister, was at that time a captain of a company in the Haganah. He once came to consult with Abba. "We found cans of preserved meat "bully beef" [canned meat] in the Russian Compound which the British left behind. Is it permissible to eat it?" Abba, who understood the problem of a company captain who struggled between the desire to keep kosher and the concern that the hungry soldiers would be simply unable to fulfill their duties, answered that it was permissible to eat it. However, whoever did not want to should not be forced to do so. Abba even found a way to permit temporary burial of the dead within the city of Jerusalem in a time of duress, "for it's possible to say that the special holiness of Jerusalem, where we do not bury the dead, expires when the majority of her inhabitants are non-Jews."

We can learn about Abba's stance with regard to establishing the Jewish state in the land of Israel from the wording of the prayer Abba composed on the eve of the declaration of Israel's independence. It is possible to infer his goal of supporting the fighters and forging unity and harmony between them and the *charedim*. The historical importance of this document is evident because it came from the great *beit din* of Jerusalem and from the lips of a *charedi* rabbi of great stature, such as my father. That being said, I won't deny that much of what happens in the state today would certainly anger my father very much indeed.

ABBA WAS CONSIDERED ONE OF THE GREAT *POSKIM* OF his generation and was described by Rabbi Shaya Chashin, head of Yeshiva Talmud Torah Etz Chayim in the early 30's as "a walking *sefer torah* (Torah scroll). *Halachic* questions from throughout the Jewish world reached him and many rabbis learned in his house, which was in truth "a gathering place for the wise." And this is how the judge of the high *beit din* of Jerusalem, Rabbi Waldenberg described him, "The rabbi's learning was measured and clear and his teachings were carefully examined. He taught clearly on the spot without hesitation, but never with haste, God forbid, but due to the fact that his reasoning had already been prepared."

Once some of the "notables" of Jerusalem wanted to test him and sent him a "fabricated question," and he immediately responded: "Such as question never existed and could never come up!" When the situation demanded it, he could be quite tough: He once ruled against one of the movers and shakers of Jerusalem, whose name I won't mention. The man asked him, "Aren't you afraid?" Abba answered, "I am quite afraid, but not afraid of you, but rather the Master of the Universe."

Abba decided thousands of judgments, wrote innumerable articles and *kol koreh*, [proclamations] gave speeches and composed warnings that dealt with all aspects of Jewish life. A portion of his countless writings (responsa and new torah insights) have been published in the anthologies of *Har Zvi*, and *Mikdash Melech*, which were published by the Machon Harav Frank in Jerusalem, led by Rabbi Shabbtai Rozenthal, the son of Rabbi Yitzchak Rosenthal, who served for decades as Abba's personal secretary.

On the Rabbinate and Politics

In 1935 city elections were held in Jerusalem, based upon the model of district elections, which was the British practice. There were two or three candidates and the rabbinate in Jerusalem, even though it did not get involved with the elections directly, preferred the candidacy of a respected businessman and native Jerusalemite, Eliezer Pearlman, who didn't belong to any party. *Agudas Yisroel* nominated a candidate who shared their approach, Shmuel Eden, the head of a *kollel* (a high level yeshiva) and, of course, an "*Agudas Yisroel* man." The members of *Mapai* (a socialist political party) had their own candidate.

The *Agudas Yisroel* men deliberated and suggested a joint political venture with their sworn enemies, the *Mapai* people: The residents of the *charedi* neighborhood of Sha'arei Chessed would vote for a Mapai man, and the residents of the Geula neighborhood, most of whom were secular, would vote for *Agudas Yisroel*. Moshe Balui, the leader of *Agudas Yisroel* in Jerusalem, who represented the extreme *charedim*, including *Neturei Karta,* [note from Avraham Frank: *At that time Neturei Karta belonged to Agudas Yisroel. Only in 1935, after the elections, did the Neturei Karta separate from Agudah, with the claim that the party was not upholding its self-proclaimed separation from the general Jewish Zionists in Israel. Since then its people remain a community of charedi Jewish extremists who oppose Zionism and do not recognize the State of Israel in terms of its institutions and laws*] strolled about the street arm in arm with Yitzchak ben-Zvi, one of the *Mapai* leaders who later become the second president of the State of Israel, calling out: "For the unity of Israel!" and tried to encourage the residents to choose their candidates.

My father was not involved in politics and was disgusted by the party leadership that, in his opinion, lacked honesty and integrity. Therefore he openly supported the candidacy of Eliezer Pearlman, a man who belonged to no party. Rav Kook also joined him in supporting this candidate. But the two of them were no match for the sophistication and political alliance between *Mapai* and the *charedim*. Eliezer Pearlman lost by only eight votes. I too was active in these elections and the results were a bitter lesson. Since then I have fled from politics as from a fire.

Abba told me that one day while he was in his office, four prominent Jerusalemites suddenly appeared. He was quite surprised and feared that a calamity had occurred, but the four, all party men, said that they came to commend a man about whom Abba was to render a decision the next day. My father listened to them and said: "I need to sit down this evening, to read all of the arguments, weigh the testimony and reach a decision by tomorrow morning. And you already can advise me of the legal decision?!" The men were chagrined and went out the way they came in. There was no love lost between my father and the Jerusalem politicians.

TWENTY-FIVE YEARS AFTER ABBA'S DEATH I MET ONE OF HIS outstanding rivals, someone who had been an all-powerful member of the *Knesset* (Israel's parliament) from *Agudas Yisroel*, Menachem Porush.[30] This was on the eve of Rosh Hashanah, 1985, when Malkah and I returned to live in Jerusalem. We had already sold and emptied our apartment in Tel Aviv, but the Jerusalem apartment wasn't ready yet. So our children arranged for us to stay in the Merkaz Hotel which, as will become clear, was owned by Porush. Over *yom tov* Rav Porush mingled with the hotel guests and when he saw us he immediately came over and, with a beaming face, said: "Avraham Frank, how are you?" The two of us were native Jerusalemites, almost the same age, both students at the Etz Chayim Yeshiva. During a conversation about this and that Porush made a revealing comment: "All of my life I fought against your father, and only in the last eight years of his life did I get to know him personally. Only then did I grasp what a great personality and *posek* he was. I understood then how greatly we had erred and what fools we were to fight him."

---

30 Rabbi Porush died February, 2010 at the age of 93. He had served as a member of the Israeli parliament from November, 1959 until June, 1994 (with a two year break from 1965-1977). Former prime minister Shimon Peres of the labor party eulogized him. In 1932, when he was barely 16, Porush was expelled from the Etz Chayim yeshiva for unseemly conduct at a Purim party when he reportedly slighted Rav Kook. http://www.jpost.com/JewishWorld/JewishNews/Article.aspx?id=169385

Chapter Two

My Childhood in Jerusalem

Mother Nursing in *Kishle*
(a Turkish prison)
Or
The Severe Famine in Jerusalem During the First World War

The Turks, who ruled the entire eastern basin of the Mediterranean Ocean for 500 years, joined the "Central Powers" (Germany and the Austria-Hungarian Empire) during World War I. The *Yishuv* (the Jewish population in the land of Israel) mostly supported the Allies (Great Britain, France, Russia, Italy and the United States). Primarily for this reason, following the Balfour Declaration, in which the British government announced that it "views with favor the establishment of a national Jewish homeland in the land of Israel," Jamal Pasha imposed curfews and harsh restrictions on the inhabitants of the land in general, and the Jews in particular: *Aliyah* to the land was stopped and the *Yishuv* was cut off from its financial resources outside of Israel. The economic condition of many Jews in the Land of Israel, in particular those whose support came from the Allies, became quite dire.

At the height of the war, during the days of severe famine in Jerusalem, my sister Sarah became ill and died.[31] She was only 17 at her death. Four months later, on May 16, 1917, I was born. Following the custom of the time, Imma gave birth to me at home with the assistance of a midwife. In honor of my *brit milah*, my parents sold a few household items and used the money to buy chick peas to serve the guests who were hungry for bread. That's the way it was.

With the advance of the British force moving north from the Suez Canal, [note of Avraham Frank: *including three battalions of recruits from the Yishuv and worldwide Jewry, the Hebrew Brigades*] the Turks issued an expulsion decree against all inhabitants who were British or American citizens, with the claim that they needed to remove a fifth column and spies from the front lines. Most of the Jews were deported to Damascus, Syria. Others fled to Egypt.

As I mentioned, when my grandfather went to America at the beginning of the century he acquired American citizenship, and so we, his descendents, were also considered American citizens and the expulsion decree applied to us as well. Imma, however, did not agree to leave the land. She well knew the dangers of attacks upon those who traveled

---

31 By the time the British defeated the Turks in the spring of 1918, the Jewish population in *Eretz Yisrael* had dropped from 85,000 to less than 55,000; between 8,000 and 10,000 had died of hunger, illness or exposure. Sachar, Howard, *A History of Israel*, (New York: Albert Knopf, 1976), 113. Yehoshua Ben Arieh quotes descriptions that appeared shortly after the war: "The crisis in Jerusalem was part of the general crisis that hit the land during the war, but in Jerusalem it was much worse." "Indescribable suffering passed over the Jerusalemite community during the First World War." Ben Arieh points out that the Jewish population growth in Jerusalem during the decades preceding World War I was not accompanied by fundamental changes in the social and economic structure of the community. So they were particularly vulnerable when the war cut off the regular *halukah* payments. Ben Arieh, Yehoshua, *Ir B' re'i Tekufah (A City As Seen Through an Era: Jerusalem in the 19th Century)*, Jerusalem: Yad Yitzchak ben Zevi, 1977), (Heb.), Vol. 2, p.571.

to Damascus, especially at this time, while she was caring for 11 children (the parents of my wife, Malkah, were also American citizens, and were likewise deported to Damascus, which I will describe later).

Courageously, knowing that violating the decree would put them in great danger, my parents decided to split up. Abba, who was in danger of immediate deportation, hid in a cave in the village of Silwan, above the Spring of Shiloah in Jerusalem for three months while Imma stayed home with the children. Occasionally Imma would secretly bring him books and bits of bread. As the front drew closer and Silwan became even more dangerous, Abba moved to another hiding place on a rooftop in the Old City of Jerusalem. The Turks searched for him, and when they couldn't find him they arrested Imma, a common tactic of the Turks. They took the women as hostages in order to pressure the men to turn themselves in. But Imma sent a message to Abba that he should stay hidden and went by herself to imprisonment in *Kishle*, the prison at the entrance to the Old City of Jerusalem, next to King David's Tower.[32] I was then seven months old and still nursing.

Imma sat imprisoned in the police station, along with about 30 other women. My sisters would bring me a few times a day so she could nurse me. In the meantime, rumors spread that the British were already at Sha'ar Ha'Gai (at the foot of the Jerusalem hills) and the women believed that Jerusalem would fall into their hands within a few days and they would be freed. But then a few German battalions arrived

---

32 "Kishle" is an Ottoman term for "barracks." It was used as a prison during Ottoman times, as well as by the British during the Mandate period and the Jordanians until 1967. Although it is adjacent to the Tower of David Museum, by the Jaffa Gate, the museum has been unable to expand into the area until extensive archeological excavation is completed. It is the site of one of King Herod's palaces. http://www.myrova.com/index.php?/content/view/313/36/

to reinforce the Turks and delayed the inevitable outcome.

One evening, shortly before Hanukah 1917, Imma whispered to my sister, Nechama, then 17 years old, "Don't bring the baby to the prison tomorrow. I'm planning to escape and you must run away from the house, because they'll look for me there."

That night before they went to sleep Imma told her fellow inmates, "I'm leaving tomorrow. Whoever wants is invited to join me." In the morning she and a few of her friends approached the gate. The guard stopped them and asked, "Where are you going?" "To the automobile, they're waiting for us outside!" Imma said confidently and without batting an eyelash. The Turkish guard was convinced that they were being released, opened the gate and the women ran outside. Imma told everyone to run to run in a different direction and not one of them was caught.

Not much later six Turkish soldiers arrived at our house in Battei Machse to search for the escapee. When my sister, Nechama, saw the Turks, she started trembling and screamed loudly. The neighbors who heard her shouts joined in with curses and yells and the Turks fled the neighborhood.

Shortly thereafter, in December, 1917, the British captured Jerusalem. The Jews of the city greeted them with blessings and took a deep breath. Abba and Imma returned home. Chanukah came. Despite the grim economic conditions, Imma found some olive oil in the house and Abba lit Hannukah lights. At that holiday the family felt that that in our home was yet another miracle of the cruse of oil, and that we experienced miracles, wonders and salvation, as it is written: "That You did for our forefathers in those days and in our time."

The Jerusalem of My Childhood

In the Jerusalem of my childhood there was no running water in the homes. Rain water was stored in cisterns that had been dug in nearly every courtyard. At the end of the summer, when the water in the cisterns had been used up, the residents used to bring water in large cans or water skins from the Spring of Shiloah, across from Yad Avshalom. The water would be kept in a *tanza* (a large earthenware jug). In order to strain the water from all kinds of filth, they would tie a thin white cloth over the jug and pour the water through it.

The grown ups used to bathe in the *mikvah* (ritual bath). The children would bathe in a tub, and when they were all finished, the water was used to wash the floor. Water was always a precious resource in Jerusalem. Imma told me that in 1895 there was a drought in Jerusalem. No rain fell all of that winter and the cisterns completely dried up. On *Shabbat ha-Gadol* before Passover, when everyone returned from the synagogue, thunder and lightning began. On that day a powerful flood came down and by morning all of the cisterns were filled to the brim.[33]

---

[33] In her memoir, Puah Shteiner describes watching their Arab neighbor pull water from the cistern. "Sometimes, while watching Abu Ali draw the water, my imagination would run free. Holding my breath, I waited for him to pull up the rope, wondering what he might find in his pail. Perhaps a fish? Or a frog? Perhaps some long lost treasure? Abu Ali would tug with his right hand, and then his left, again and again until once more he would be holding a pail, overflowing with water. But it was always only ... water! 'What did you expect to find in a water cistern?' my grandmother once asked me, noting the disappointed look on my face. 'Uh ...' I stammered, 'maybe something that was once lost ... maybe a ... a treasure ...' She laughed. 'Water is the greatest treasure there is,' she said, carefully balancing her full pail, not spilling a drop. I only realized the truth of Savta's words during the war, when this treasure became very scarce." Shteiner, Puah, *Forever My Jerusalem*, translated by Bracha Slae (Jerusalem: Feldheim, 1987), 21-22.

Imma, The rebbetsin Gita Malka, a"h

When Imma did laundry, she used the water several times (as we would say today, "recycling.") First of all, she would heat coals and boil water in a *fillah* (a large container). First she would wash the bedding, the tablecloths and the whites, and then she would use the same water to wash the dark clothes, and when she finished rinsing, she would add starch to stiffen the fabric,[34] she'd wring and hang the laundry and then use the rest of the water to wash the floor.

In my childhood there were no kerosene stoves in Jerusalem, no refrigerators, no ice, and, of course, no electricity. There was no way to keep food for any amount of

---

[34] Dodah Esther told me that one cold day her father returned home hungry and helped himself to a bowl of soup from the pot on the stove. He received a scolding from his wife—the "soup" was starch for laundry.

time. Every day we bought milk, boiled it and drank it that day. When there were holidays lasting a few days, like Rosh Hashanah, the custom was to put the food in a tin can and lower it into the water cistern in the courtyard. Before the meal one of the children would be sent to pull up the rope holding the container, and so milk and fresh food could last through the holiday.

In honor of Shabbat Imma used to bake *challah* (braided white bread) and prepare the Shabbat meal: fish, soup and meat. When strangers happened to come to the city, they were also invited as guests to the meal. On Shabbat we ate *cholent*, (a traditional stew of beans, eggs, barley and meat) which cooked in a pot over coals all night. Occasionally Imma would prepare egg salad or different baked goods. First she'd spread out the flour, add water, knead it and then roll out the dough. Then she'd cut it into strips when she made noodles, circles when she made cookies, and squares when she made *kreplach* (meat filled dumplings) for the soup. I never liked *kreplach*. At our house we joke that we make them only in some connection to some kind of beating: at the eve of Yom Kippur when the *shamash* (a synagogue functionary) would [gently] hit the worshippers; Purim, when we remember Haman; Hoshanah Rabba, when we beat the willow branches, or when the housewife isn't sure whether to throw out the leftover meat. She'll think it over, finally smack herself on the head and make *kreplach* out of it.

In Jerusalem they used to pickle vegetables and olives, and preserve fruit. In the summer Imma would buy fresh cucumbers and pickle them. Then a tinsmith would come to the house to salt and seal the containers. These were placed in the cellar and remained closed until Purim. Imma would also buy apricots and other fruit during the summer and would make jam out of them.

At sunrise Abba would wake up the boys for *shacharit* prayers. Imma got up even earlier in order to light the coals and put up the kettle. When we returned from the prayers the water was boiling and she poured hot tea for us all.

Every morning the bread delivery man would leave two loaves of bread at our doorstep. One morning Imma got up late, but in time to see someone snatching the bread and running away. That day we were hungry and the children didn't get even a bit of bread for school. But on a regular day, we would go to school with a sandwich with a little halva or a small piece of cheese. We had to make do with that for five or six hours. When we came home, Imma would give us *shirs mit brite* (a piece of bread spread with olive oil heated in a frying pan), sometimes sprinkled with salt with a piece of cucumber or tomato. In the evening, after *ma'ariv* (evening services), we ate salad. And if we had some extra income, Imma cooked soup that had bits of meat. Once in a while we were lucky enough to have fruit. I don't remember hunger in my childhood, but it was certainly a difficult life. That may have been the reason that when I grew up I decided to be independent, to work in manufacturing and take care of my family.

Our shoes were repaired over and over again and passed along from one pair of feet to another, from one child to another until they completely fell apart. Holes in socks were patched, as were the clothes. We all accepted this as natural, nobody complained. This was the life of most of Jerusalem's population.

THERE WERE ONLY A FEW CARS IN JERUSALEM IN THOSE days. In 1918 the distinguished Jerusalem *maggid* (preacher), Ben-Zion Zeisling brought to Jerusalem one of the first automobiles ever seen in Israel.[35] My brother Tanchum, z"l, told me that many curious people gathered to see the wonder and to admire "the horseless carriage." By the way, that same Ben-Zion Zeisling was the grandfather of the first minister of agriculture in the State of Israel, Aharon Zeisling, one of the heads of the *Kibbutz Ha-meuchad* and one of the founders of Kibbutz Ein Harod.

During the Jewish holidays an atmosphere of holiness would descend upon Jerusalem. I looked forward to them longingly, each holiday with its rituals, special foods and unique character. In particular, I loved Sukkot and Pesach, because for these holidays sometimes we'd get new clothes or new shoes. For Sukkot each family would make colorful paper chains to decorate the sukkah. But the other holidays were also special: On Chanukah Abba would light the candles with the entire family gathered around; on Tu B'Shevat they would try to get as many different types of fruit as possible so that we could make the blessings over them; on Purim we'd dress up in costume and deliver *mishloaḥ manot* (food gifts), at least two treats in each basket, and during the Purim feast we sang special songs for the holiday. We used to sing the following song in our home and every year my family asks me to sing it to them:

---

[35] Rabbi Zeisling was an unusual personage. He was a rabbi in Vilna, strict in his observance, and an expert in German literature. He translated Schiller into Hebrew and was a poet in his own right. His collection of secular books was kept under lock and key—he followed the precept of "know how to answer the apostate." He moved to Jerusalem in 1905. Tidhar, p. 2922. A *maggid* is a rabbi who focuses on preaching.

I will take this cup in my hand
Joy, happiness and cheer withstand
La, la, la

Blessed is God in His speech
Blessed are you God, Creator of each
La, la, la

Even if wine is expensive
Still my drinking would be extensive
La, la, la

I'll speak my words with a nod and a wink
And with a smile I'll swallow my drink
La, la, la

Praise God that we have wine
If we drink it, all will be fine
La, la, la

Oy, oy to the heavens I'll cry
Diluted wine? I say, "Fie!"
La, la, la

This is what I get from all my work
My fate is this cup, I shall not shirk
La, la, la

A long peaceful life I will attain
For in one gulp this cup I'll drain
La, la, la

Wine has a wonderful fruit flavor
Good for the kidneys, if you savor
La, la, la

[Translation with whimsical license]

Immediately following Purim the preparations for Pesach began: we'd clean and whitewash the house. As the holiday approached the Passover utensils were taken out of the storage place, the *shemurah matzas* (specially prepared *matzah*) were brought from the bakery, we searched for *chametz* (leavened break) and removed it. At the appointed time the entire family gathered, dressed in holiday clothes, to the Seder table. The entire *haggadah* was read, carefully and in depth, we sang the holiday songs, and we feasted as one should. On the night of Shavuot, the holiday of the giving of the Torah, we learned until dawn and after Shacharit services we ate blintzes and then went to sleep.

Our neighbors, the Arabs of the Old City, were quite familiar with the Jewish holidays and even gave them nicknames. The Arabs called Yom Kippur, *Eid-al-Gaz*, the holiday of the chickens, because of the custom of *kapparot*.[36] They called Tisha B'Av *Eid-al-Gazoz*, the soda holiday, because at the end of the fast, which took place at the height of the summer, the worshippers would return from the Kotel to the Jewish Quarter, and would buy soft drinks to quench their thirst.

THE PHARMACIES OF MY CHILDHOOD DO NOT RESEMBLE today's pharmacies at all. I'll give you an example with this story: One morning, when I was about 15 years old, Imma asked me to bring some medicine to Savta. My grandmother, Malkah Frank, my father's mother, lived with us at that time and that morning she hadn't felt well. I went to the pharmacy, whose shelves were filled with bottles of ground

---

36 *Kapparot* is a custom of symbolically transferring one's sins onto a chicken during the days leading up to Yom Kippur. Riding on the bus through Meah Shearim I'd see "*Kapparot* stands" set up on the sidewalk.

herbs, dried greens, and strange and mysterious items. It wasn't like today, where medications come packaged and already prepared. In those days the pharmacist himself prepared the medication.

The pharmacist, an elderly Jew named Feivel Leibel, asked me, "And what can I get for you?"

"*Savta* doesn't feel well," I answered.

"Wait a moment and I'll prepare a medication for her," said Mr. Leibel. He didn't ask for particulars about her symptoms, nor did he ask to see the sick woman, rather, he simply began to crush up herbs and a few other things, added a little of this and a little of that, mixed it all together and finally wrapped up the strange smelling powder in a piece of paper. Then he brought out a small bottle containing a yellowish liquid and instructed: "Tell her to swallow two teaspoons full of the powder twice a day with water, and one teaspoon of this once a day after eating," pointing at the liquid.

Savta had no questions or doubts about any of this; the pharmacist's medication was enough to strengthen the body and revive the spirits. I don't know what Mr. Leibel prepared for her, but she became stronger and got well. She died three years later, in 1935.

WHEN IMMA ASKED ME TO DO SOMETHING SOMEHOW I didn't always seem to notice. Sometimes she needed to repeat her request several times. "Avraham, the roof is leaking, go up on the roof and replace a tile," or "Avraham, fix the dripping faucet," and so on and so forth. On the other hand, if Abba asked something, or even said a word I immediately jumped to do what he asked. I saw that he was absolutely authoritative, more so than any man I've met before or since.

In 1941 Abba was hospitalized for an operation in the Assuta Hospital in Tel Aviv. Imma was with him all day and I stayed by his side at nights. One day I heard the head nurse speaking to the nurses in German, nodding her head in my direction, "There's a young man who paces like a tiger. If you are careless, or if something doesn't work properly here, we're sunk!"

On Saturday night my brothers, Yaakov and Yehudah, came to relieve me. Abba was surprised and asked, "What happened? Did Avraham get tired?" "No, we just thought we'd let Avraham sleep one night," they answered. "As long as he is quiet, leave him with me for the night shift," Abba said with a smile. Two weeks later, when he was released from the hospital Abba said to me, "Now you can take a rest," and that's what I did.

When I was still a lad in Jerusalem a young Jewish policeman by the name of Yitzchak Tunik came to the Old City. Many people were thunderstruck. Why on earth would a Jew join the Mandate police? It turned out that he had been recruited by the Jewish Agency, which oversaw the Jewish *Yishuv* in Israel, in order to integrate the British police force. Thirty years later we met in Tel Aviv. I remembered him well, but he didn't remember me, since I was just one of the city kids. Tunik was surprised and happy when I told him that I knew him from the time when he was a policeman in the Old City. He was a good friend of my brother-in-law, Rabbi Gronum Lando, my sister Mina's husband, and he used to visit him on Shabbat to learn a page of *gemara* together. Later on Tunik studied law, established a thriving law office and became one of the influential lawyers in the State. In 1982 he was appointed as state comptroller and the commissioner for public complaints (ombudsman).

THE DAILY SCHEDULE FOR ALL JEWISH CHILDREN IN THE Old City was identical: *Shacharit* services at sunrise, then study at a *cheder* or *talmud torah*. *Mincha* services were in late afternoon and then in the evening we'd return to the synagogue for *ma'ariv*. We didn't waste time, nor did we have much free time. When I grew older and turned to the business world, Abba was reconciled to my chosen path, but in every letter that he wrote to me he urged me to set aside some time for reading and study: "I know that you are very much tied up with work, but dedicate a little time for study, *chumash* and Talmud …"

In the early 1950's a young man came to my factory in Tel Aviv. The son of a *sofer* (scribe) in Jerusalem, Yaakov wished to work for me. I hired him but two months later he got sick and was told that he needed to have his appendix removed. He asked for 25 lira to pay for the operation and hospitalization, a substantial sum in those days. I gladly gave him the money, wished him a full recovery and never saw him again. It turned out that he passed away after the operation. Half a year later a young woman came to see Abba. She introduced herself as Yaakov's sister and said that the day before he died he asked that they repay the debt to Avraham. She worked, saved money and now she was returning it. Abba said, "Take half of this money for yourself, and give the other half to *tzedakah* in your brother's memory."

Abba told me of those instruction and added, "I did this in accordance with your spirit," and he was correct in that. The education in giving *tzedakah* and helping those in need was so deeply rooted in our lives and worldview that there was no need to say another word.

And if we're talking about *tzedakah*, I would be remiss if I didn't mention Aunt Pesha, my father's sister and her great *middot* (good characteristics). Pesha was married to Yitzchak Gavrilovich, the grandson of Eliezer Dan, one of the prominent men of Jerusalem in his time. In 1914, when the famine in the land was at its height, Yitzchak and Pesha decided to try their luck in Chicago in the United States. They did well in business (which included, among other things, dealing in liquor during the "dry era" in the United States). Despite this success, they suffered from the strong arms of the Chicago underworld; the gangster Al Capone, head of best known organized crime group in America demanded protection money from them. In the middle of the night, the Gavrilovich's left the lights burning in their home, fled America and returned to Israel.

Yitzchak Gavrilovich returned a prominent businessman and began to deal in real estate. He bought large lots of land, particularly in Tel Aviv and his family was well provided for. During the time of the great depression, the city of Tel Aviv requisitioned some of these lots for public purposes. One of these was the large section upon which stands the cultural hall and the Habima Theater. Despite this, Gavrilovitch remained a well to do man. My Aunt Pesha, for her part, completely devoted herself to *tzedaka* and generosity. Abba used remark that, "Of all the charitable people I have known, there were never those more righteous than Pesha and Yitzchak Gavrilovich." They donated generously to support Torah scholars, to provide for brides, and, in general, to all the city's poor. One of their sons-in-law, a Haganah member, Dani Gelmond, was active in bringing in Jewish immigrants illegally. Aunt Pesha set up the cellar of her home to accommodate many refugees and took care of all their needs. Six of them actually became household members. Aunt Pesha helped them find jobs, financing their weddings and their settlement in the land.

In 1954 Yitzchak Gavrilovich died and Aunt Pesha set aside the rental income of an entire building to distribute among outstanding yeshiva students, in memory of her husband. This enterprise continues to this day. My father, z"l described Aunt Pesha in these words: "She had a genius for *tzedakah*." On the sixth of Av, 1975, Aunt Pesha passed away. A eulogy that I keep in an album in my home says, among other things, "An important and great woman, who bestowed goodness and not evil all the days of her life … and her good name went before her throughout every corner of the land."

Battei Machse

The construction of Battei Machse began in 1860. The initiative to build this neighborhood, the only Jewish neighborhood established within the city walls, were the men of the "Holland and Germany" Kollel. They persuaded the heads of the *Pakuim* Organization (the Clerks and Administrators in Amsterdam) to set aside money to buy the lot and to build houses. The neighborhood was built on a large lot on the southern edge of the Jewish Quarter, which was registered in the name of Yosef Peretz, a Sephardic Jew who had since died. The consuls of Prussia and Austria were brought into the secret of the purchase, since they were the ones who could guarantee the transaction in the Turkish registry office. [Note by Avraham Frank: *Regarding the property transfer to the Kollel of Holland and Germany, Zev Vilnai, one of the leading researchers of the history of the Land of Israel, and the father of General Matan Vilnai, told a story that the Arabs placed guards at the Turkish registry office to prevent the business from going through. On Yom Kippur the guard didn't show up, because it didn't occur to them that ownership would transfer on that day, but it was precisely then that the business was concluded. According to a leniency granted by the rabbis (on the condition that a non-Jew would write it at the direction of the Jews), as is written in the Babylonian Talmud, Tractate Gittin, page 8b,* "*one who buys a field ... as a buyer in the Jerusalem area ... who writes it even on Shabbat .. because of the mitzvah of settling the Land of Israel*]

Once the lot was purchased, they needed to gather the building funds. With this goal in mind they published a *kol koreh* (proclamation) throughout the diaspora explaining the great need to establish the neighborhood; emissaries went out to fundraise throughout the world, even going so far as America and Australia. It wasn't just Jews who contributed. Even Franz Joseph, the Kaiser of Austria-Hungarian Empire, gave 1000 franks, and the southern gate of the neighborhood is named for him "Joseph's Gate." In 1862 Azriel Havisdorf, the contractor, completed building the first apartment in the neighborhood.[37]

---

37 Havisdorf came to *Eretz Yisrael* in 1847 from Hamburg, Germany. His trip took about 60 days by sailboat. While en route a terrible storm arose and the boat's captain asked Havisdorf to pray to his God, like Jonah the prophet. Havisdorf prayed and blew a shofar and soon thereafter the storm subsided. This created

Battei Machse in the old city. Our home was the arched building on the right, and that's where I was born.

It was agreed that the neighborhood's residents would rotate every three years, since the apartments were rent free for poor scholars. Seventy-six apartments were erected in the neighborhood, and five were reserved for visitors. One third of the apartments were given to the people of the Holland-Germany Kollel, a third to the Hungarian Kollel and another third for the remaining groups.

One of the outstanding enterprises in the neighborhood

---

great respect for Judaism among the crew members. After he settled in Jerusalem, Germany and Austria sent consular representatives to the Holy City and Havisdorf, as a German speaker, became the spokesman of the community. He worked with Charles Netter in purchasing land for Mikveh Yisrael, the first agricultural school/colony founded under Jewish auspices. He provided leadership and used his many connections in Europe to raise funds on behalf of the Jews of Jerusalem, and helped found institutions such as the Diskin Orphans Home and Misgav Ladach Hospital. Of his 13 children, three survived. They received a Torah education and were tutored privately (and secretly) in secular subjects and languages. He died at a ripe old age in 1905. Tidhar, p. 2354-55.

was the "hospitality house," for visitors who came to Jerusalem for a short time or those who were moving to Jerusalem and needed temporary housing until they could establish themselves. In the guest book of the "hospitality house" you can find names such as: "Rabbi Shmuel Salant, Rabbi Adler, the chief rabbi of London, and other notables from around the world.

A Zeppelin in the Skies of Jerusalem

The Zeppelin above the streets of Jerusalem, Adar 1929.

On Purim, 1929, in the middle of the *megillah* reading, I heard some talk in the synagogue about "something" flying in the sky. We went to the synagogue roof and we saw a giant balloon floating above us. It was the Graf Zeppelin that arrived in the land of Israel. [Note by Avraham Frank: *Count Graf von Zeppelin (1838-1917) was a German aviation pioneer. Following discharge from his army service in 1890 he set out to build rigid air ships that are, to this day, named for him. Zeppelin acquired the blueprints of a Croatian Jewish engineer, David Shwartz, who, in 1896 built a prototype of an airship, but died before he was able to fly it. Zeppelin continued to develop the idea and created it as an elongated sphere filled with hydrogen and equipped with engines and propellers.]* It left Germany, flew across the world, reached Jerusalem, circled the Temple Mount, was illuminated by spot lights and continued on its way around the globe.[38]

Regarding Four Synagogues in the Old City

The Churvah synagogue.

---

[38] The New York Times described the Zeppelin's arrival in Tel Aviv during Purim: "The Zeppelin was lowered sufficiently to enable the gay, cheering throngs, most of whom were picturesquely costumed, to read plainly the airship's name. At different places in Tel Aviv small bags were dropped containing mail, addressed mostly to Germans. The dirigible then headed toward Jerusalem Although arriving in the dark, she circled over the Holy City for a full hour. Turbanned Moslem sheikhs, gazing from rooftops centuries old, cried: 'Allah may thy name be praised; how great are thy wonders.'" New York Times, March 27, 1929. Since Purim in Jerusalem is celebrated one day later than the rest of the country (Shushan Purim) the Zeppelin would have been over Tel Aviv during Purim day and then over Jerusalem for the megillah reading there that night. And since Purim is in the middle of the lunar month, there would have been a full moon, making it easy to see.

The Churvah Synagogue

"Churvat Rabbi Yehudah He-Chassid," or "the Churvah," for short, was an Ashkenazi synagogue, the most ornate in the Old City. In 1921, when I was a four year old boy, Abba took me one Shabbat to this synagogue, where he used to pray on *shabbatot* and holidays. About a year earlier Herbert Samuel had been appointed as the first British High Commissioner for the land of Israel. He was also the only Jew who was ever appointed to this position. Before coming to Israel he held several high positions in his homeland of Great Britain, serving in parliament and as a cabinet member. In Israel Herbert Samuel lived in the Commissioner's House in the vicinity of Augusta Victoria [hospital] which was between the Mount of Olives and Mount Scopus. (The building served as the dwelling place of the high commissioner from the beginning of the British Mandate, 1920-1927, until the construction of Armon Ha-Naziv on the "Hill of Evil Counsel.")

That year, on *Shabbat Nachamu*, which follows Tisha B'Av, Sir Herbert Samuel was invited to the Churvah synagogue. He arrived on foot from his residence and was called up to the Torah for the *maftir* section (for the *haftara* reading from the prophets). The synagogue was full of the worshippers' whispers. A festive atmosphere surrounded them, and they were filled with high spirits, as if the days of the Messiah had arrived. The excitement grew and intensified when the high commissioner began to read the twofold consolation of the prophet Isaiah: "Be comforted, be comforted my people." Many tears were shed. I was a little boy and didn't understand the *haftara* nor the significance of the occasion, but the exhilaration that gripped the crowd did not escape me.[39]

---

39   Herbert Samuel's popularity among the Jewish population of Israel was short-lived. Ironically, his commitment to impartiality led him to overcompensate for

The Churvah Synagogue was one of the most beautiful in Jerusalem. Its doors were cast of steel, engraved with flowers and leaves. The doors were created and donated by a Jew in Moscow. In those days it was important to Russia to demonstrate its interests in the Middle East and when the doors set out on their journey to Israel, they were accompanied with great pomp; Czar Nicholas sent his royal band to the Moscow train station to play at the farewell ceremony for the delegation leaving for *Eretz Yisrael*.

In the large sanctuary of the Churvah stood a beautifully crafted *aron kodesh* (holy ark) that reached about 20 meters high. On the *bimah* (platform) were four large marble columns, which had been brought on 14 camels from the port of Jaffa to Jerusalem. The flag of the "Hebrew Brigade"[40] was kept in a special cabinet in the synagogue; the soldiers of this brigade, who fought during World War I as part of the British Army, entrusted it to the custody of the Churvah.

A seven-branched silver oil menorah, resembling the menorah that stood in the temple, had been donated to the Churvah by a Jewish tailor in Moscow. They say that he was the court tailor who sewed suits for Czar Nicholas. A captain, whose measurements were the same as the czar's would come to try on the suits and only when the suits were almost completed would the suit be sent to the royal palace for the final fitting. One day, after the captain had finished the fitting and gone on his way, the tailor felt something strange in the pocket of the suit. He reached in and found a grenade with which the captain and his friends

---

his personal convictions as a Jew and a Zionist. His decision to severely limit Jewish immigration deeply disappointed Zionists in Eretz Yisrael and abroad. Sachar, p.125.

40 The Jewish Legion was founded by Zev Jabotinsky as part of the British army in World War I in Palestine. Their participation in the defeat of the Ottoman army was an important component of Jewish claims to the land. Sachar, 113-115.

had intended to assassinate the czar. The tailor hurried off to warn the czar, which resulted in a large cash reward. The tailor used this money to order the menorah and then donated it to our synagogue.

In the courtyard of the Churvah was the famous Etz Chayim Yeshiva. As a child, my first years of study were spent at the *talmud torah*, like an elementary school today, which was attached to the *yeshiva* and also located in the Churvah courtyard. In 1925, when I was about eight, the synagogue was being replastered. Suddenly, while we were deep in study, the ladders toppled, fell on the *bimah* and smashed it. By great fortune nobody was injured. At that time Abba served as the rabbi of the synagogue, the *gabbai* was Amdorski, the cantor was Ben-Zakkai, and the *shammash*, Shlomo Freiman (who kept the key for Rachel's Tomb in Bethlehem, from the time of the Turks until the War of Independence).[41] With the help of donors and congregants the necessary funds were gathered and the *bimah* rebuilt.

One morning in 1927, when I was about ten, we were sitting in class with our teacher, Rabbi Chaim Menachem Mendel Mendelson, in Etz Chayim. Suddenly we heard a deafening noise that shook and rattled the building. It was a powerful earthquake.[42] "Children, get outside!" the rebbe yelled. All of the children of the Etz Chayim Yeshiva, including me, ran outside where, of course, the grown ups joined us. There were those who cried out that the Mount of Olives was about to split, as was prophesied at the time of resurrec-

---

41 The dual position of *shamash* at the Churvah and at Rachel's Tomb was held by three generations of Freimans; Shmuel Freiman was sixth generation in Eretz Yisrael. Tidhar p.3068. His son, Yehoshua (Shuki) Freiman was actively involved in the rebuilding of the synagogue, which was completed in March, 2010. *Jewish Action*, Fall 2010.
42 The 1927 earthquake registered 6.3 on the Richter Scale and was centered near Jericho and killed 200 people. http://www.msnbc.msn.com/id/3980139/ns/technology_and_science-science/t/jerusalems-old-city-risk-earthquake/

tion of the dead. All of us were stunned and quaking in fear. The roar continued and the ground beneath us continued to shake. We saw walls swaying and cracks spreading in the ceilings and walls around us. Many houses in the Jewish Quarter were damaged. The Chabad synagogue was damaged, and many Arabs died. No one among the Jews was injured, and the *talmud torah* and the Churvah Synagogue remained secure on their foundations.

The *gaon* Rabbi Michel Tukochinski, the head of the Etz Chayim Yeshiva, whom I mentioned as Abba's *chavruta*, sent workers to repair the cracks. They attached iron braces by way of long screws to the *yeshiva* walls. But even these repairs didn't reassure us. For many weeks after the earthquake we sat in class quivering with fear and unable to free ourselves of the memories of that terrible noise.

In the *talmud torah* next to the Etz Chayim Yeshiva I was fortunate to learn with gifted, knowledgeable and intelligent teachers. We were about 20 students in the class and I was the most mischievous one of them all. Studying was not my primary interest, but I am proud to describe the intellectual achievements of some of my classmates. Reb Yosef Cohen, who later married the daughter of my brother, Tanchum, was a bright and diligent student. His father owned a flour mill in the old Yemin Moshe neighborhood.[43] Reb Yosef achieved greatness and became a judge in the high rabbinical court in Jerusalem. His son, David, serves as

---

43 Yemin Moshe and Mishkenot Sha'ananim were among the first Jewish neighborhoods built outside the Old City of Jerusalem. It was named in honor of Moses Montefiore, one of the very important Jewish philanthropists of that era who changed the landscape of Jewish Jerusalem. One of the features of the neighborhood was a windmill. It is a commonly held belief that the windmill never functioned as a mill, but that view is being reassessed. Until the reunification of Jerusalem in 1967 this neighborhood literally sat on the border between Israel and Jordan and only the very poor lived there. After the war it was rebuilt and renovated and became a highly desirable place to live. www.jerusalem.muni.il.

head of the Hevron Yeshiva in Jerusalem. Baruch Rackover, the grandson of Reb Simcha Mandelbaum, for whom the Mandelbaum Gate was named,[44] was appointed as a judge in the rabbinical *beit din* in Haifa. Yaakov Shachor, the grandson of Reb Ze'ev Shachor, an importer of medicines during the First World War, was also a classmate of mine. Yaakov Shachor studied chemistry and became the head of the chemistry department of the Institute for Testing and Development of Medical Materials in the Health Department. Yishayahu Goldschmidt, who came from Lithuania with his father, was a devoted student and more refined than the *sabras*, born in Israel. He was later appointed as rabbi and judge in the rabbinical *beit din* in Tel Aviv. Moshe Hamburg served as the head *shochet* (religious slaughterer) in Tel Aviv. Benyamin Kosovsky also learned with me. He was the son of Rabbi Chaim Yehoshua Kosovski, the author of the concordance, *Otzar Milim Targum Unkelos*.[45] I remember visiting Benyamin's house and always seeing his father engrossed in his writing. Asher Ettinger also learned with me; he was the grandson of Reb Leib Benziman. I will also mention Mendel Wagshal, a classmate of mine who later became a promoter of the *Me'am Lo'ez* books, originally written in Ladino, which contained stories, commentaries,

---

44 The Mandelbaum Gate served as a border crossing between Israel and Jordan between 1948 and 1967. "All this has grown out of the informal conferences ten years ago by the Israeli and Jordanian army commanders in Jerusalem. They began meeting between the lines in a ruined house once owned by a man named Mandelbaum ... In January, 1950, Rafael Levy, assistant district commissioner of Israeli Jerusalem, began meeting at the gate with International Red Cross representatives and Jordanian officials to locate families separated in the Arab-Israeli fighting. As the months went by there were other problems arising out of the sudden partition of Palestine. Soon Mr. Levy began going to the gate three times each week to meet a Jordanian with similar duties." *New York Times*, February 21, 1959.

45 He created a concordance for the *Mishna* by developing a mathematical algorithm which permitted a more efficient method of processing the information (he had published mathematical research in his younger days). Tidhar p.831

laws, *midrashim* and traditions of the Jews of Spain. Reb Yaakov Koli began this great undertaking, but he wasn't fortunate enough to complete it. After his death the enterprise was finished by Mendel Wagshal and others and it became a permanent possession of the Sephardic Jewish heritage. Yitzchak Salant also learned with me, the grandson of the well known maggid of Jerusalem, Natan Netta Weiss, who, sadly, died at a young age.

THE CHURVAT RABBI YEHUDAH HE-HASSID SYNAGOGUE, or "The Churvah" for short, was built on the ruins from the construction attempts of Yehudah Halevi He-Chassid, a rabbi who lived in Poland at the end of the 17th century. He was a kabbalistic rabbi and preacher who foresaw that the final redemption was near and decided to move to *Eretz Yisrael* along with a group of his followers. The pious rabbi went around to towns and villages and called upon Jews to move to Jerusalem in order to hasten the coming of the messiah. The procession he led numbered several hundred men, women and children. Along the way to *Eretz Yisrael* their numbers grew smaller and smaller so that by the year 1700, when the group arrived in Jerusalem, there were only 300 people. Rabbi Yehudah he-Chassid managed to buy land in order to build a synagogue for the Ashkenazic community in the city. (The Sephardim had their own synagogues which were called collectively by the name of Yochanan ben-Zakkai.) But the day after purchasing the land and signing the contract to build the synagogue, Rabbi Yehudah became sick and on the third day of his illness he passed away, leaving his group of followers like sheep without a shepherd.⁴⁶

Despite this, the construction of the synagogue began. However, it progressed slowly due to lack of funds. Because of the debts owed them, Arabs attacked the synagogue one Shabbat and wrecked it. The Ashkenazic Jews were accused of withholding wages from Arab workers and they were all forced to leave the city. The Muslims would chase after any Ashkenazic Jew who crossed their path, each one of whom they considered personally guilty. Things got to such a point that an Ashkenazic Jew approaching Jerusalem would put on a *tarbush* (also known as a fez, a distinctive Ottoman hat) in order to pass as a Sephardic Jew.

The Muslims maintained their hold on the Churvah for more than 100 years, and throughout that time the Ashkenazic Jews tried to redeem it. In 1836 they finally succeeded, and got a permit to rebuild. In 1850 Rabbi Zalman Tzoref⁴⁷, grandfather of Yoel Moshe Solomon, one of the

---

46 Yehudah Ḥassid Halevi, ca. 1650-1700, was a popular mystical teacher and kabbalist. Although he never publicly embraced Sabbatianism (followers of the false messiah, Shabbetai Zevi (1626-1676) see note 67), many of his followers and supporters were avowed Sabbatians. His group of pietists resolved to move to the Holy Land to await the imminent arrival of the messiah. In 1700 on Shabbat Hagadol before Pesach, Yehudah he-Ḥassid delivered a sermon in Frankfurt am Main proclaiming that within a year there would be no more Jews or Christians in Frankfurt. Approximately 1,600 Jews set out on this journey. Many died along the way and only 1,000 arrived in Jerusalem. They had already purchased land in the city, but were unable to sustain themselves financially, especially without the charismatic leadership of their rabbi, who died six days after arriving in Jerusalem. The Sephardic community was openly hostile towards this group, in part because of the suspicion of Sabbatianism. When the messiah failed to arrive most of the pietist group returned to their countries of origin; some embraced Christianity or Islam in their disillusion. Maciejko, Pawel. 2010. Yehudah Ḥasid ha-Levi. YIVO Encyclopedia of Jews in Eastern Europe. http://www.yivoencyclopedia.org/article.aspx/Yehudah_Hasid_ha-Levi

47 Avraham Shlomo Zalman Tzoref came to Eretz Yisrael from Lithuania in 1811. While on the journey he learned to become a silversmith and set up a successful shop in Safed. An outbreak of typhus in 1812 forced the family to move to Jerusalem. Other Ashkenazi Jews came from Safed to Jerusalem, although they had to keep that secret from the Muslim population. Eventually, they were able to gain recognition. Tzoref's efforts to regain the Churva meant that some Arab families were forced to move (with compensation), which appears to be the reason for his murder. Tidhar, 45-46

founders of Petach Tikva, began to rebuild the synagogue, but was murdered by Arabs. In 1852 the Churvah again lay in ruins, until 1857, when new foundations were laid by the builder Reb Hillel Sherlin. The construction took a long time—again due to lack of funds—until gradually contributions from Israel and abroad were gathered. The synagogue was finally dedicated in 1864 in the company of Sir Moses Montefiore and Baron Alphonse d'Rothchild whose contributions made up for the construction costs. Later on the building was further improved by the addition of an enormous dome, which rose above the rooftops of the Old City of Jerusalem.

The ornate synagogue stood for 84 years and served a spiritual home for all the Jews in Israel. Next door to it stood the important and great Torah school, Etz Chayim, which was established in 1841. Every day many hundreds of children learned in its *talmud torah*, and older students learned in its *yeshiva*. For the 70 years he lived in Jerusalem, Rabbi Shmuel Salant, the legendary rabbi of Jerusalem, resided there and until World War I, it was the site of the city's high rabbinical court. In 1901 it was the location of the memorial service for Queen Victoria. The synagogue was new and exquisite, but retained the name *Churvat Rabbi Yehudah he-Chassid*, in memory of the man who led the group of immigrants who first built it.

During the War of Independence the Churvah was destroyed. Its large dome and upper walls were toppled. After the Six Day War, when I returned to the Old City, I looked for the synagogue and found only ruins.

This was not the only synagogue that was destroyed. The Arabs wrecked dozens of other synagogues in the Old City. Today you can see just one of the arches which supported the dome. The arch was reconstructed after the Six Day War.⁴⁸

The Ramban Synagogue

Adjacent to the lot where the Churvah Synagogue was built was the Ramban Synagogue, which had been built 400 years earlier. The Ramban, Rabbi Moshe ben Nachman (1194-1270) was one of the great Spanish scholars, a *posek*, commentator, leader, kabbalist and physician.⁴⁹ He came to *Eretz Yisrael* in 1267 and established a synagogue in Jerusalem in the cellar of a building that had been neglected and abandoned, and had clearly served some other purpose previously. Until the arrival of the Ramban, Jewish Jerusalem had been in ruins for around 170 years. During the time of the Crusades all of the Jewish institutions in the city had been destroyed and the Jewish inhabitants were murdered or fled. The Ramban lived only three years in Jerusalem, but during that short time he brought about a turning point in the history of the Jewish Yishuv in *Eretz Yisrael*.⁵⁰

For a certain period of time the ownership of the Ramban Synagogue passed from Jewish to Arab hands.

---

48   One arch was built after the Six Day War to mark the location of the synagogue. The Churva was recently rebuilt and dedicated March 15, 2010. http://www.jta.org/news/article/2010/03/15/1011107/police-secure-jerusalem-for-synagogue-rededication
49   In 1263, the Ramban was ordered to participate in a public disputation in Barcelona with a well known Jewish apostate, Pablo Christiani. (These so-called debates were designed to disprove Jewish theology and strengthen Christian belief) When the four-day disputation was over, Rabbi Moshe had clearly won and was banished from Spain soon thereafter. He made his way to Jerusalem, but then settled in Acre. He wrote one of his greatest works, his commentary on the Torah, while in Eretz Yisrael. http://jewishencyclopedia.com/articles/12552-ramban
50   During the Crusader period the Jewish quarter was in the north-eastern area of the city (where the Moslem quarter is today). The emergence of the current Jewish quarter, in the south of the city, can be dated to the Ramban's decision to establish his synagogue in this area—near the Kotel, with a view of the Mount of Olives. Ben-Arieh, Vol. I, p. 357

And this is how it came about: The building next door to the synagogue belonged to a Jew who, because of a financial dispute with Jewish partners, converted to Islam. His mother followed his example and dedicated her home, which adjoined the courtyard of the synagogue, for the construction of a mosque. Indeed, the calls to worship of this mosque are still heard today, just steps away from the Ramban Synagogue, in the heart of the Jewish Quarter. After the mosque was built the Arabs tried many times to seize the synagogue from Jewish hands, but they were unsuccessful and the Jewish inhabitants of Jerusalem continued to pray in it and even got permission to renovate and improve it. Finally, in the 16th century the Arabs managed to take over the synagogue that was so close to a mosque. For the nearly 400 years or so the synagogue's holiness was gone, and its historical importance faded with the passing generations until it was forgotten entirely. It became a factory for small cheeses, raisins and so forth. It was only after the War of Independence [sic][51] that the synagogue was identified and renovated with great taste by the "The Company for Rebuilding the Jewish Quarter in the Old City of Jerusalem."[52]

The Witty Comment That Helped Complete the Construction of the Tiferet Yisrael Synagogue

The establishment of the Tiferet Yisrael Synagogue in the Old City of Jerusalem, named for Rabbi Yisrael of Ruzhin, also took many years due to lack of funds. The followers of

---

51 After the Six-Day-War.
52 The location reverted to Jewish hands in the mid-19th century and then was destroyed after the 1948 War of Independence. It was renovated and rebuilt after the the 1967 Six Day War. http://www.jewish-quarter.org.il/atar-ramban.asp

Rabbi Yisrael of Ruzhin, led by Nissan Bak, an acronym of *Ben Kedoshim*, (son of holy ones), finished the construction in 1876.[53] Nissan Bak was the son of Yisrael Bak, a remarkable man, a book publisher from Berdichev, Ukraine came to Eretz Yisrael in 1831. Yisrael Bak first settled on Mt. Jermack (Mt. Meron) near Safed and established the first Hebrew printing press in Israel in 400 years. (There was a printing press operating in Safed in the 16th century for a brief time). Members of his family joined him: five of his daughters, his only son, Nissan[54] and a few other Chassidic families from Berdichev and Odessa.

After their homes and property, including the printing shop, were destroyed by rampaging Druse, Yisrael Bak moved the printing press to the city of Safed itself. But in 1841, four years after the powerful earthquake that hit Safed, Yisrael Bak moved to Jerusalem with his family.[55] He

---

53 Yisrael of Ruzhin (1796—1859) was an unusually flamoyant Hassidic leader during the time of Hassidism's greatest growth. He founded a new style of Hassidism, "the regal way," wherein the rebbe/tzadik would live an opulent lifestyle. His palace was known for its carriages and thoroughbred horses and a *klezmer* band accompanied him when he traveled. He and his followers maintained that only the Tzaddik could follow the regal way without enjoying its material benefits. Through his well endowed Volhynia kollel fund, he was able to influence Hassidic groups in Jerusalem and Safed. Assaf, David. 2010. Yisra'el of Ruzhin. YIVO Encyclopedia of Jews in Eastern Europe. http://www.yivoencyclopedia.org/article.aspx/Yisrael_of_Ruzhin

54 In 1833 the 17 year old Nissan Bak led the group of about 90 immigrants. During the journey aboard a sailing ship, one of the women gave birth, and Nissan Bak performed the circumcision. The drunken ship's captain revealed his plan to sell his passengers as slaves. When they anchored near an island in the Aegean Sea, Nissan made his way to the local Turkish ruler and revealed the plot, thus saving their lives. Tidhar, p. 64.

55 In 1834 the Druse in the Gallilee region rebelled against Ibrahim Pasha. They attacked the Jews of Safed. After the rebellion was put down, Ibrahim Pasha was stricken with malaria. He heard of a Jewish healer in Safed, Yisrael Bak, and sent for him. With Bak's help Ibrahim Pasha recovered and Bak was rewarded with the title "Chakim Bashi," "The Pasha's Physician." According to family legend, his life was saved during the great earthquake because an Arab peasant begged him for medication and delayed him in the house, which kept him from attending *minha* services. The earthquake hit during the services and the worshippers were buried alive. Some say that the unknown peasant was really the prophet Elijah. Tidhar, p.59-60.

established a new printing shop with an advanced new press that Sir Moses Montefiore sent him as a gift.

Yisrael Bak was the uncrowned leader of the Chassidic community in Jerusalem, had close relations with the Turkish ruler, and was, for a while, the Wallachian consul in *Eretz Yisrael*. In 1843 he acquired the lot upon which he intended to build the Tiferet Yisrael synagogue. His son Nissan, who inherited his father's involvement in communal activities, took upon himself to oversee the construction of the synagogue. Nissan's connections with the government were also excellent, and the Pasha even wanted to name him Chacham Bashi, leader of the community, but Nissan Bak turned down the honor in order to retain his Austrian citizenship. The Tiferet Yisrael synagogue was built between 1859 and 1873 under the close supervision of Nissan Bak, who also served as architect and engineer, consulting from time to time with the architect who built the Russian Compound.[56]

In 1869 the Suez Canal was opened with a festive ceremony. Among the high ranking guests who attended the ceremony was the Kaiser of the Austria-Hungarian Empire, Franz Joseph, who ruled during two generations of the monarchy, then at the height of its power. On his way to Egypt, the Kaiser passed through Jerusalem and visited his

---

56 The Russian compound was built from 1860-1872, a time when there was a building boom in Jerusalem. It is a large compound made up of many buildings centered around a Russian Orthodox cathedral. It was built to serve the many Russian Orthodox came to Jerusalem on pilgrimage. In addition to the church it included a hospital, hostels for pilgrims, offices for religious and consular officials and large cisterns. The church had 10 domes which were painted green and dramatically visible. It was also the first church in Jerusalem to have cathedral bells—until then the Ottoman government had forbade the use of bells in church in order to protect Muslim sensibilities. The church was dedicated in 1872 in the presence of the Russian prince Nicolai, who came to Jerusalem along with a retinue from the Czarist court. Ben-Arieh, 105-6. Today, as in the time of the British Mandate, it is used as a police station and jail.

Austrian subjects. The notables of Jerusalem came to greet him, including Nissan Bak, who hosted him and invited him for a short stroll in the streets of the Old City. And now we get to the story of how the Tiferet Yisrael synagogue was completed. The building stood upon its foundation, but had no dome. The Kaiser asked, "Why doesn't the building have a roof?" and Nissan Bak impulsively answered, "The synagogue removed its hat to honor his majesty!" The Kaiser burst out laughing, asked how much it would cost to dress the synagogue with a hat, and donated the necessary sum.

In 1876 the work was completed, and the beautiful synagogue was dedicated. It stood until 1948. The Jordanians completely destroyed it after they captured the Jewish Quarter.

Grandmother Susil Friedman, Malka's paternal grandmother, who walked arm in arm with the Rebbetsin at the funeral of her husband, the Kalisher Rav.

A Short Story About the *Parochet* (ark curtain) in the Synagogue of the *Perushim* in Battei Warsaw in the New City (outside the Old City walls)

There is a strange and mysterious larger than life story about this *parochet*, a tale that began in 1860, when Rabbi Meir Auerbach, called The Kalisher Rav, came to Jerusalem. Rav Salant appointed him as a judge in his *beit din*. It was The Kalisher Rav's bad fortune to be married to a shrewish woman who tormented him and embittered his life. One day, when he had had enough, the rabbi could no longer restrain himself and angrily "blessed" her: "You will never earn the right to be buried in a Jewish grave."

The Kalisher Rav died in 1878, and two years later the friends who remembered him went to visit his grave. Of course his wife, the *rebbetsin*, went with them, walking arm in arm with Susil Friedman, grandmother of my wife, Malkah. They recited some chapters of psalms, left a rock on the grave, and then the group started to walk towards the exit. The *rebbetsin* was no longer there. She disappeared as if the earth had swallowed her up. People searched for her as far as Jericho, but were unsuccessful. To this day the riddle remains about the disappearance of the *rebbetsin* and the words of her husband were fulfilled: his wife was not buried in a Jewish grave.

AND IF WE'RE TALKING ABOUT MYSTERIOUS STORIES, I'LL tell another tale I heard in my childhood. In 1900 an event took place in Jerusalem: a man was buried alive. And this is how it happened: The man, married and the father of three young children, became ill, stopped breathing and was declared dead. As was customary in Jerusalem, the men of the *chevra kaddisha* (burial society) came the same day, and conducted his funeral and burial. That night in a dream, the woman saw her husband saying, "They buried me alive! They buried me alive!" and again the next night, and the third night. On the fourth night she saw her husband lying on his side and his fingers torn up with his attempts to dig himself out of the grave. When she told this to Rav Shmuel Salant, the rabbi told the members of the *chevra kaddisha* to open the grave and they were horrified to find the deceased lying on his side, his fingers covered with wounds.

AFTER THE SIX DAY WAR I RETURNED TO THE OLD CITY for a visit. I was among the first group that received permission to visit the city, on the first day its gates were opened for civilians. It was heartbreaking to see the ruined synagogues. One synagogue was even used as a donkey stable, and cow barn, others were demolished and forsaken. Only one synagogue remained standing, Beit Chabad, which was used as a residence. So in 2005 I had no illusions about the decision to leave behind the synagogues in Gush Katif (in Gaza). I knew that the Arabs would leave no trace of them.[57]

But in the summer of 1967, when we met the Arabs of the Old City, they greeted us happily. They told us that the situation under the Jordanian rule had been dreadful and bitter, that they had to pay bribes for every step they took, until they felt imprisoned in their own city, under an extended occupation. A Jewish man in our group met an Arab childhood friend, who grew up with him in the Old City. They embraced and cried and we were all quite moved. We thought that messianic times had arrived. I looked for Mussa, an Arab storekeeper who sold charcoal in the Old City. For many years his family used to buy *chametz* from my mother's grandfather. He always complained that he had seven daughters and only one son. "Where is Mussa?" I asked. "He passed away some time ago," they answered. I remembered that Mussa's only son became a Muslim sheik

---

57 Hours after Israel officially ended its rule over the Gaza Strip, Palestinian Authority bulldozers began to pull down synagogues left behind by the evacuated Israelis. Other synagogues in Gaza were torched. Haaretz.com/print-edition/news/Palestinians-torch-gush-katif-synagogues-1.169652 9/13/05.

and I went to the mosque to search for him, but I didn't find him. While we were still wandering in the city an elderly Arab woman approached us and began to speak a fluent Yiddish. She remembered all of the Jewish families who lived in our neighborhood, and she fondly recalled her former neighbor, Feiga Ettel Rokovski.

Sha'arei Zedek Hospital, or "Wallach" Hospital

Wallach Hospital was established after a major dispute regarding control of the Jewish hospital Bikkur Cholim in Jerusalem. A group of *charedim* who came from Germany started to build their own hospital under the protection of the German Kaiser. The efforts didn't go well at first; the turning point came with the arrival of a young *charedi* doctor, Moshe Wallach, who had been sent by the Jewish communal council of Frankfurt. Dr. Wallach began his medical work in the Old City in the guest house in Battei Machse. Soon thereafter he opened a clinic and pharmacy on Armenian Street in the uppermost section of the Jewish Quarter. The young and energetic doctor went to Germany to collect funds and obtain the imperial German endorsement for building a hospital. In 1894 Wallach succeeded in gathering enough money to buy a lot outside the city walls where a hospital could be built.

The new hospital was designed by the German engineer and architect Sandler, who was also the architect of the German hospital in Jerusalem. The plan included building a wall surrounding the lot and digging cisterns to collect rainwater. The great distance between the new hospital and the Old City and Jewish residential centers raised concerns that patients wouldn't go to this hospital; sharp words went about the community that Dr. Wallach would have to compensate patients for their transportation costs.

The construction of the hospital began in 1896, by the Jewish building contractor Reb Ya'akov Mann. The news reporters of Jerusalem gave details on the improvements and upgrades that were incorporated into the building (an elevator, running water) and on the cooperation between Jewish and Arab workers in the construction, that the Arab workers were experienced trained workers, and the Jews were learning from them. The building plan authorized by the Jewish council in Frankfurt included three buildings: A two-story central hospital with a basement for storage and medicine; a secondary building which would serve as a residence for the medical staff; and a hospital for patients with chronic diseases. These three buildings were to be surrounded by a large garden. Creating a garden around a hospital was unprecedented in the *Yishuv* and added beauty and grace to the compound.[58]

The editor of the newspaper *Ha-hashkafa*, Eliezer ben Yehudah,[59] noted that the new hospital was the most beau-

---

58 Shaarei Zedek Hospital moved into a more modern facility in 1979. The old building is a designated historical landmark and is now used as the headquarters of the Israel Broadcasting Authority. www.szmc.org.il/NewsHighlights/OriginalHospitalBuildingReceivesProtectedStat/tabid/1432/Default.aspx

59 Eliezer ben Yehudah (originally Perlmann) is considered the father of modern spoken Hebrew. He was born in 1858 into a Chabad Chassidic family. His father died when the boy was five years old. After his bar mitzvah his mother sent Eliezer to her brother's home in Polotzin, where he enrolled in a small local yeshiva. The head of the yeshiva was secretly a *maskil* (enlightened one who studied secular subjects) and introduced Eliezer to *haskalah* literature. The boy's uncle found out and was furious and sent him elsewhere. But that didn't help. At the age of 15 Eliezer announced to his mother that he was going to attend gymnasia, the high school. While enrolled in medical school in Paris, and while continuing his involvement in Zionist and Hebrew causes, he became ill with tuberculosis and had to move to a warm climate. In the winter of 1881, with the support of Baron Rothschild, he went for treatment in Algiers, and there he learned to converse in Hebrew with the local Sephardic Jews with the Sephardic pronunciation. He married Devorah, whose father had mentored him in his

tiful one in Jerusalem, and even today it arouses wonder and deserves to be preserved. At the opening celebration in 1902 all of the notables of Jerusalem participated: the leading rabbis, representatives of all the various *kollels*, the Turkish pasha, the German consul and high ranking Turkish bureaucrats.

The hospital was called *Sha'arei Zedek*, named for the Jewish neighborhood that was built next to it, and Dr. Wallach was appointed director and chief doctor. Dr. Wallach's persona was so dominant that everyone in Jerusalem just called it "Wallach Hospital." Dr. Wallach linked his destiny with the hospital and led it with great wisdom. During World War One, when the financial support of the German Jews was temporarily suspended, Dr. Wallach gathered fruit and grew vegetables on the hospital grounds in order to provide food for patients and staff. When he died, Dr. Wallach was buried in the small cemetery next to the hospital, and was praised as one who lived out the verse, "You shall love your neighbor as yourself,"—an acronym of his name.

Another resident of the hospital was Selma Meir, the head nurse and an important personality in her own right. She was called "Shvester Selma," ("Nurse Selma"). She was

---

youth, and they moved to Israel, vowing to speak only Hebrew. In Jerusalem he gave up his Russian citizenship and his Russian name, going only by his Hebrew name of Ben Yehudah. He was so stubborn on this point that he turned down a check for 100 rubles because it was made out to his Russian name. When his son Itamar was born he went to great lengths to ensure that the child would never hear a language other than Hebrew. In 1891 Devorah died, leaving him with two young children. His doctors gave Ben Yehudah six months to live with his tuberculosis, and recommended that he not remarry. Again, in his stubbornness, he defied them and asked Devorah's younger sister Beila if she would come to Jerusalem and marry him and be a mother to her deceased sister's children. She agreed and they married the following year. Eliezer ben Yehudah had many disagreements with the religious establishment in Jerusalem over the years, as well as with secularists. He died in 1922, not long after the British Mandate declared Hebrew an official language. Tidhar, pp. 1612-16.

childless, but within the hospital she raised children who had been abandoned by their parents.[60]

Abba underwent an operation at Wallach Hospital in 1959. At one in the morning they took him out of the recovery room and I thought he was still groggy from the surgery. To my astonishment he suddenly said, "Avraham, now I clearly remember my involvement in Wallach many years ago." So, at an hour when the rest of the patients were sound asleep, with a light shining only at the nurses' station, I sat at his bedside and he told of a quarrel that broke out between Dr. Wallach and Ya'akov Mann, the contractor who built the hospital. Reb Ya'akov Mann had a one-of-a-kind personality in that he was not only a successful contractor, but was also a learned Torah scholar.[61] He and Dr. Wallach had agreed on the terms and had a signed contract that the hospital would be completed within five years, and the payment was set accordingly. But the contractor had managed to complete the construction in three and a half years. Dr. Wallach didn't know what to do. The payments were based on collecting donations, and there wasn't enough money to pay him at this point. They turned to Abba, who found a way to straighten out the problem.

"What was your decision?" I asked. And he answered: "I

---

60 Schvester Selma Meir was an important personage in Jerusalem. She arrived from Germany in 1916 and "quickly turned 'Dr. Wallach's Hospital' upside down in her efforts to impose German standards of cleanliness and order." After six years in Jerusalem she returned "home" to Hamburg for an extended vacation, but after three months she felt the tug of Shaarei Zedek and returned to Jerusalem to stay. An orphan herself, she adopted two daughters. "She walked away from work for the first and only time when one of the girls was killed in a terrorist attack on Ben Yehudah Street." She was the head nurse at Shaarei Zedek until 1964 and died in 1984, two days short of her 100th birthday. http://www.szmc.org.il/NewsHighlights/Servicewasherlifeandherjoy/tabid/951/Default.aspx

61 Rav Yaakov Man taught at the "Degel Torah" school and was offered as position as rabbi and judge. However, he refused to support himself through Torah study and went into the family building business. He was the first Jewish contractor in Jerusalem. He arranged classes in *mishna* and *gemara* for his workers. Tidhar, p. 1029

don't recall the particulars, but I found a solution that left both parties satisfied."

The Events of 1929

On Friday, August 23, 1929 the riots broke out. In Jerusalem the agitation among the Arabs could be felt already by midday. They stormed out of the mosques in processions and loud shouts.[62] There were confrontations between Jews and Arabs in some of the alleyways of the Old City. In the meantime it became clear that with the British turning a blind eye and maintaining their silence, the Arab rabble planned to enter the Jewish Quarter by way of Zion Gate. A few young men from the Haganah set out to protect the Jewish population. They included Shimon Furman, Ya'akov Berger, who died later in Chanita, Eliyahu Ettinger and Itzik, whose last name I can't recall. They shot in the air and managed to prevent the Arabs from entering the Jewish Quarter. When these young men saw the British approaching they quickly fled from the area to Battei Machse so that their weapons wouldn't be confiscated. Imma said, "Leave the weapons with us and hide somewhere else!" The weapons were hidden in our house, Imma set the table for Shabbat and we even had guests. It happened that on that Shabbat Yosef Avidar[63], the head of the Haganah, had been invited to the meal. Years later he would remind me the wonderful Shabbat meals and the holy and festive spirit that always enveloped our home.

---

62   For the first six months of 1929 there had been Arab protests against Jewish prayers at the Kotel (the Western Wall). Escalating tensions led to an attack by "crowds of Arabs on individual, unarmed Jews in the Old City of Jerusalem." Gilbert, p.60

63   Yosef Avidar was born in Ukraine in 1906 and moved to Israel in 1925. With the establishment of the State Avidar was one of the first officers in the IDF and served as head of the quartermaster branch and as officer of the northern and central regions. After his discharge he served as ambassador to the Soviet Union and then Argentina. He died in 1995. Noted in the text.

The next day was the *brit milah* for Ya'akov, my brother Tanchum's son. My older siblings, Ya'akov, Yehudah, Pesha, Rachel and Minah went to the ceremony at the Wallach hospital. Along the way Arabs shot at them and they hit the ground and escaped without injury. On the way home some Haganah men met them, saying with concern and amazement: "It's enough that you managed to reach Wallach, but to come home safe and sound to Battei Machse—that's a real miracle!"

It wasn't until Shabbat was over that we learned about the massacre that took place against the Jews of Hevron, including relatives of ours: On that terrible day, the 18th of Av 5689, 28 members of the Slonim family were murdered in Hevron, including my Aunt Yenta, Abba's sister, her husband, Rabbi Ya'akov Orlinski, their daughter, Channah, son-in-law, Eliezer Dan, and their five-year-old grandson, Aharon. Only the one-year-old baby, Shlomo Slonim, survived despite being slashed in the head by a knife. (Shlomo Slonim grew up, had a family and today lives in Ra'anana. He still bears a scar on his forehead that the knife blade left behind.)

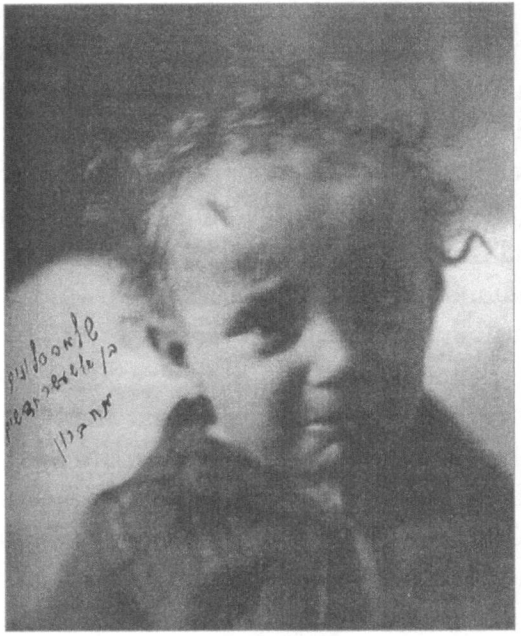

Shlomo Slonim, the sole survivor of the young Slonim family.

My Aunt Yenta, Abba's sister, was married to Rabbi Avraham Ya'akov Orlinski, the rabbi of Zichron Ya'akov; he was the son of the first rabbi of Petach Tikva, Rabbi Aharon Orlinski. On the 15th of Av 5689 they married off their daughter, Rachel, to Ya'akov Bronstein-Brosh. Their eldest daughter, Channah, invited the family to come to Hevron for Shabbat so they could celebrate *sheva brachot* (week long celebrations following a wedding). Channah was married to Eliezer Dan Slonim, the son of Rabbi Ya'akov Slonim, the rabbi of Hevron. My Aunt Yenta and her husband traveled to Hevron, but the young couple was stuck in Tel Aviv and sent a telegram saying that they'd have to delay their arrival because there were no cars going to Jerusalem. This saved their lives. My brother,

Ya'akov's life was also spared. He was learning in a *yeshiva* in Hevron, but Imma insisted that he come home for the *brit milah* of our brother, Tanchum's, son, Ya'akov.

Seated: Rabbi Avraham Yaakov Orlinski, the rabbi of Zichron Yaakov; his wife, the Rebbetsin Yenta Orlinski, nee Frank, my father's sister; their five year old grandson Aharon Slonim; Standing: Their daughter, my cousin Channah Slonim and her husband Eliezer Dan Slonim. Our relatives who were murdered in Hevron.

About 70 Jews had gathered in the Slonim house, hoping to find refuge there. Its owner, Eliezer Dan Slonim, director of the Anglo-Palestine Bank and leader of the city's Ashkenazic community, was known to have good relations with the Arabs, and was respected by them, since the family was native to Hevron.

One of the notables of Hevron, Nasser el-Din, a friend of Slonim, was among the first to burst into the house. One day earlier he had promised to protect him and his family from the bloodthirsty rioters, but when the moment of truth came, he was their leader. The survivors, who feigned death, described in horror the shouts of five-year-old Aharon Slonim, "Nasser el-Din is killing me!!" After a few moments the boy's voice was silenced. He was badly wounded and died in Jerusalem.

The family members who were buried in a communal grave in Hevron on the evening of the 20th of Av were: Avraham Ya'akov Orlinski, 49, rabbi of Zichron Ya'akov, murdered while still wrapped in a *tallit*, where the room still echoed with the words from the priestly blessing at the end of the musaf service: "And bring you peace;" his wife Yenta Orlinski, Abba's sister, 47; Eliezer Dan Slonim, 30, director of the Anglo-Palestine Bank in Hevron; his wife, my cousin, Channah Slonim, daughter of Rabbi Orlinski, 27; and their son, Aharon Slonim, 5.

Rabbi Ya'akov Slonim and his family survived thanks to their landlord who protected them, one of the few who came to the rescue. A greater tragedy was averted, thanks to about 10 Arabs, among the righteous people of the world.

Until the massacre, around 600 Jews lived in Hevron, and they had good relations with their Arab neighbors. Sixty-seven Jews were murdered in the 1929 massacre, which brought an end to the continuous Jewish presence in Hevron.

After the massacre, Rabbi Ya'akkov Slonim moved to the Zichron Moshe neighborhood and was the *baal tekiah* (*shofar* blower) for the neighborhood synagogue. To this day I can hear him reciting the blessings before blowing the *shofar*, "From the depths I call out to You, God," he'd recite, and your heart was torn in sorrow. His daughter Rivka Slonim married Dr. Yosef Burg, z"l, and was the mother of Avraham Burg, who became the head of the Knesset.

The riots spread to other areas throughout the land. After three days the British mounted a show of force and the disturbances in Jerusalem ended. However, they continued in other parts of the land for an entire week, during which more than 130 Jews died and hundreds were wounded.

Chapter Three

Growing Up

DIFFICULT YEARS

In 1930 we moved from Battei Machse to live in the Kerem Avraham neighborhood, outside the walls of the Old City.[64] My sister Nechama, who lived in America, sent a sum of money and Imma used it to buy a lot on 14 Malachi Street. Imma supervised the construction and Abba, as always, dealt with legal matters and learning and was completely uninvolved with building the house. One day when Imma was overseeing the Arab workers, a group of Jewish communists passed by and said: "Why are you building a house here? We are building a Jewish state in Birobidjan in Russia."[65] "Nothing will remain of Birobidjan!"

---

64   The development of Kerem Avraham was an important part of housing developments outside the old city of Jerusalem. The first house there was constructed by the British Consul, James & Elizabeth Finn. In 1855. It still stands today at 24 Ovadiah Street. Ben Arieh, 95-96. Amos Oz grew up in that neighborhood and describes it in his memoir, "Some two hundred Jews were employed on the Industrial Plantation in Finn's farm in work such as removing stones, building walls, fencing, planting an orchard, and growing fruit and vegetables, as well as developing a small stone quarry and engaging in various building trades. In the course of time, after the consul's death, his widow set up a soap factory in which she also employed Jewish workers." Oz, Amos, *A Tale of Love and Darkness*, Harcourt, Inc., 2003, p. 119.

65   This region in the Soviet Far East was designated the "Jewish Autonomous Region" by that communist regime. It was intended as an ideological alternative to Zionism. Jewish immigration began in April 1928. Of the prospective settlers who arrived between 1928 and 1933 more than half left. The purges of 1936-38 led to a deterioration of the Jewish leadership in the region. After 1948, when the

she retorted, and she never knew how right she was.

Moshe Baram, a *Mapai* man who was active at that time in the Jerusalem workers council, would go through the streets of Jerusalem calling out to contractors: "Hire Hebrew workers!" instead of the skilled and inexpensive Arab workers. The "conquest of [Jewish] labor" was a problematic issue and the worker's movement focused upon it. The contractors, of course, preferred to hire Arab workers. I don't recall who worked for us, but I well remember the legitimate fight that Jewish workers waged for their right to work.

Our house was built of stone, with a red roof and a small garden surrounding it. The plans called for two entrances, one for the public and one for the family.

In 1932, when I was 15, I was sent to learn in the Tiferet Yisrael Yeshiva on Favazner Street in the Hadar section of Haifa. I'd take the train from Jerusalem to Haifa, only coming home for the holidays. I was completely enthralled by Haifa's scenery. Like every Jerusalemite, the sight of the ocean thrilled me and in those days the train tracks came almost to the water's edge. (The construction of the port of Haifa had been recently completed and just one year later, in 1933, the port was officially opened).[66]

RABBI MEIR RUBMAN, THE HEAD OF THE YESHIVA, MAINtained a high level of learning and discipline. Most of my

---

Soviet Union moved to suppress Jewish activities, any dream of vital Jewish life there ended. Encyclopedia Judaica pp.1046-50. My father traveled to Birobidjan some years ago to see the remains of this failed experiment.

66 In 1922 Sir Frederic Palmer surveyed the coast on behalf of the British Mandate and determined that Haifa would be the best location for a deep water port. Acre had been the main port in the region for over 2000 years, but over the course of time its port had been clogged with silt. The Port of Haifa opened on October 31, 1933. http://www.haifaport.co.il/template/default_e.aspx?PageId=158

classmates were diligent students, but as for me—no. The yeshiva students lived in cottages, four to a room. One of them was Chagiz, the great-great-grandson of Rabbi Moshe Chagiz, one of the leading rabbis of Jerusalem 250 years earlier, well known for his relentless pursuit of Rabbi Moshe Luzzato, whom he accused of being a Sabbatean [a follower of Shabbtai Zvi, the false messiah].[67] Chagiz later studied engineering and became a successful manufacturer. Tzuriel from Tiberias also studied with us. He was a conscientious student and later became a rabbinic judge in Jerusalem. My friend Ibbu, whose family had lived in Safed for over 180 years, also became a judge in the rabbinical court in Jerusalem, but died at an early age. The two Grossman brothers were also classmates. Today Yisrael Grossman is a rabbi in Jerusalem, and his son is the rabbi of Migdal Haemek and is an influential public figure. His brother moved to America, was drafted into the American army and participated in the invasion of France during World War II. Another classmate was Menachem Tepperberg, born in the Old City to an old Jerusalem family. Menachem became a manager of the family vineyard, "Yakvei Ephrat" in Motza. The vineyard, founded in 1870, was the first of its kind in the modern era. Menachem Tepperberg, an energetic and industrious man, was recently honored as a *Yakir Yerushalayim* (Worthy Citizen of Jerusalem).

---

67 Shabbetai Zvi was a false messiah who lived in the 17th century. He gained many followers during a time when the Jewish world was reeling from the Chelemenitzki massacres in Poland. In 1666, after he had triumphantly proclaimed himself to be the messiah in the city of Jerusalem, he was imprisoned by the sultan and offered the choice of conversion or death. He chose conversion, devastating the vast majority of his followers. In the centuries that followed faithful followers of Shabbetai Zvi continued to hold fast to their belief in their leader. Traditionalist rabbis were on the lookout for those suspected of being Sabbateans. http://jewishencyclopedia.com/articles/13480-shabbethai-zebi-b-mordecai

I was in Haifa for only one academic year. When summer vacation finally arrived I went home. Imma saw my downcast appearance and said to Abba: "Our son is not enjoying *yeshiva*." "What does he want?" Abba asked. "To learn a trade," she answered and Abba agreed. Without Imma's support Abba would have never agreed and I would have been unable to leave the yeshiva.

There were no trade schools in the city, so I began working as an apprentice at "Ostreicher and Perel" in the Romema section of Jerusalem, which dealt with electricity and motors. The conditions of my apprenticeship were that I would work for two years without pay, but would receive payment for overtime. Sometimes we were sent to do car repairs throughout the city. They repaired machinery for Angel and Berman, the two large bakeries in the city, they installed elevators in new buildings and carried out other jobs. Most of the money I earned I turned over to Imma, and with the little that was leftover I bought, first of all, a pair of shoes and then a suit which cost two and a half lire.

At the same time I played with the idea of joining a *kibbutz*. I heard that a religious group was forming to found a *kibbutz* by the name of Kevutzat Rudgaz. These were religious youth from families in Germany who were inspired by the Zionist idea and joined a farm in Europe so they could prepare themselves for agricultural life in Israel. They were the ones who set in motion the development of religious *kibbutzim*. I went on foot from Tel Aviv to Petach Tikva, arrived at the place and saw three tents and a few kibbutz members, most of them German immigrants. I asked if I could join them but they turned me down, saying that they had no room to take in additional members.[68] Greatly disappointed,

---

68 The founders of Kevutzat Yavneh had agricultural training as a group in

I left the way I came. In 1941 the members of Rudgaz moved to land on the coastal plain, about five kilometers east of Ashdod, and established Kevutzat Yavneh, which still exists.

IN THE HAGANAH[69]

In 1934, when I was 17 years old, a *bachurnik* (dude) I knew, by the name of Malachi, came to see me at work. He was already a member of the scout movement [and was ready to move on]. "We need to enlist in the Haganah," he announced, to which I happily agreed. One dark evening Malachi and I arrived at a certain building in Jerusalem. On the table rested a Bible and we laid our right hands upon it and swore allegiance. Our commander was Yigal Yadin, who became the second Chief of Staff of the Israel Defense Force.[70] He trained us to shoot pistols and how to use Morse code.

We were called the "Young Connection Haganah Com-

Germany before coming to Eretz Yisrael. www.yavnet.org.il/maainsite. asp?sitename=kvyavne It would not be unusual for them to be reluctant to accept additional members at the outset of their settlement. Most of the kibbutzim were not religious and many were dogmatically non-religious, deliberately choosing to distance themselves from Jewish religious practices, considering them part of the diaspora. Today there are 16 religious kibbutzim. They are committed to the idea of *Torah V'avodah* (combining Torah observance with labor) and see themselves as a bridge between the religious and secular Jews in Israel. www.kdati.org.il

69 The Haganah came into being in 1920 in the wake of Arab attacks on Jews in Jerusalem. Its origins were in the Hashomer, a loosely organized local Jewish defense group. The Haganah became more tightly organized in the 1930's in response to the growing conflict with Arab groups and the lack of confidence in British protection. Shimon Peres, who later become prime minister of Israel, describes a candlelit induction ceremony with a pistol and a copy of the Bible. Tessler, Mark, *A History of the Israeli-Palestinian Conflict*, Indiana University Press, 1994. p.186

70 Yadin (originally Sukenik) was only 23 when he became assistant to the first chief of staff of the Haganah in 1939. "Yadin" was his nom de guerre. During the War of Independence he became the Chief of Staff, sometimes clashing with Ben Gurion regarding the use of limited resources. He structured the Israel Defense Force with compulsory service, which included a standing army and reserves. In 1952 Yadin went back to school, earning a Ph.D. in archeology at the Hebrew University. He then achieved great acclaim for his excavations at Hazor and Massada. Gilbert, pp.102, 196, 264-65.

pany." Hillel Fefferman, who became a contractor in Jerusalem, was with me in the company along with Moshe ben-Giat, the Mishka brothers, and Betz Rabinowitz, Yoska Harel and Yossi Yadin, Yigal's brother, and others.

The activities had an underground flavor to them. We passed along messages and recruited new members by using hidden notes. My parents knew that I had been inducted into the Haganah, and our home even served as one of the first places in Jerusalem where the Haganah's ammunition was stored.

In 1935 I was sent to a Jerusalem residence to help a Haganah member secretly prepare grenades. Hidden in his house were the components: a fuse wire that served as a detonator, and gunpowder—an entire factory! We cut the fuse wire into pieces 6 centimeters long, then we screwed a ring onto the fuse wire and we rubbed the wire its entire length in damp gunpowder. We carefully left everything to dry and two days later we put the gunpowder into the grenades. We threaded the wires upward and the grenade was ready to use. The fighters would scrape the wire against a matchbox, as if it were a match, the wire would ignite and they'd have only two seconds before the grenade exploded.

Mostly we worked in a schoolyard in Beit Hakerem. The Haganah men had hidden a large heavy machine gun there, Schwarzlose,[71] of German make, which was called "the black one." In February, 1936, we set out on foot from Beit Hakerem to conduct weapons training in the wadi next to Kiriat Anavim, today the location of the *kibbutz* cemetery.[72] There, for the first time in my life, I trained with live

---

71 This gun was developed in Austria and used extensively during World War I. http://www.firstworldwar.com/atoz/mgun_schwarzlose.htm
72 Kiryat Anavim was the first kibbutz settlement established in the Judean Hills, purchased initially in 1913, but not settled until 1920. It is approximately 12 km.

ammunition and threw a live grenade. We were an entire company, about 40 men, but there weren't enough weapons and ammunition to go around, so not everybody could practice with live ammunition. The echoes of the explosions reached the ears of the British and they appeared in the area to see what was going on. Our commander, Chiyun, calmed them down and told them that we were exploding stone in order to level the area and they left. After that we hiked back to Beit Hakerem that night. Before we dispersed our commander gave us a short lecture about safety rules, the activities planned for the future, and he told us that there was growing evidence that the Arabs were planning attacks on Jewish settlements. And so it was. Two weeks after the training, the 1936 riots broke out.

THE RIOTS OF 1936 BEGAN IN JAFFA, WHEN ARAB RUF-fians attacked Jews on the street, killing nine and injuring 57.[73] The riots continued about three years and more than 600 Jews were killed. The Arabs called a general strike in the Arab towns, the port of Jaffa and the Jewish orchards.

These events changed my life. Up until then I worked at Ostreicher and Perel, and participated in Haganah activities only when I had free time. At this point I completely abandoned the work and put my entire wherewithal into the Haganah.

---

from Jerusalem. The kibbutz served as an important defense outpost for the Haganah during the siege of Jerusalem. http://kiryatanavim.homestead.com/whoweare.html

73 The Arab Revolt of 1933-39 was characterized by strikes, violent attacks on Jews and serious clashes with the British police. During the 1936 riots described here, 80 Jews were killed and approximately 300 wounded; 197 Arabs died and nearly 1,000 wounded, the majority at the hands of British security forces. Additionally, 28 British citizens lost their lives. Jews were the targets of kidnapping and murder which triggered reprisals by the militant Irgun organization. Tessler, p.239-40.

First we were sent for basic training in Kibbutz Kiriat Anavim. Michael ben-Channan drilled us; a graduate of the first squad commander course of the Haganah, he later was dubbed "Mr. Morning Exercise." He taught us how to use weapons. As a real *Yekke* (German Jew), ben-Channan demanded order and was strict about inculcating the fundamentals of military discipline. When we finished our training we were sent to guard a Jewish village north of Jerusalem, Neveh Ya'akov, and also in the Old City.

The Haganah commander in the Old City was Ze'ev Epstein Ovnat, and his lieutenant was Nachum Gershnowitz, and under their command were also two young women: Dina Baham, and Nachum's sister, Shoshanah Gershnovitz, who later became the first commander of the Chen (the women's division) of Tzahal. The two made important contributions, hiding weapons beneath their clothes, or pretending to be innocent girlfriends walking arm in arm with their boyfriends.

Every week we were stationed at a different street in the city, with weapons hidden in our clothes. Sometimes we were sent to guard duty in public places, including "Beit Weingarten," where the Museum of the Old City is located today in the Jewish Quarter of Jerusalem.[74] At that

---

74 The Old Yishuv Court Museum http://www.jewish-quarter.org.il/atar-museum.asp tells the story of the Jewish community of the 19th century. It contains many photos and artifacts that belong to my ancestors, including a *kapota* (coat) that belonged to Rabbi Frank, and medical instruments that belonged to the "Bubbe Golde," a famed midwife in the early 1800's—my great grandmother's mother (Stampfer side). Dodah Leah Goodman, my grandfather's sister, told me that when the Bubbe Golde died she asked to be buried with long knotted rope. She said that each time she delivered a baby and the family was too poor to pay, she put another knot in the rope. Dodah Leah told me that there were over 500 knots in that rope. She was also a highly regarded healer. My mother said that she was told that a British doctor went with Bubbe Golde on her excursions to pick medicinal herbs, so that he could learn. Dodah Leah also told me a story that once the Bubbe Golde met a woman at the kotel who was weeping bitterly. "What is wrong?" she asked. The woman explained that her daughter was very ill. My great-great-grandmother said, "There is a woman here, they call the Bubbe

time Beit Weingarten was the house at the farthest edge of the Jewish Quarter, and from there it was possible to look out on what was happening the Muslim Quarter. For this reason Haganah men gathered there, including some who later became public figures, like Moshe Baram, Minister of Transportation in the Israeli government and Aharon Katzir, who became a professor of physics at the Weizman Institute and was killed by Japanese terrorists in Lod Airport in 1972.[75]

In the wake of the 1936 disturbances a Jewish religious battalion was established in the Old City under the command of Shimon Agassi. Many yeshiva students were recruited, including: Yitzchak Epstein, who became a judge in the Tel Aviv beit din, Yankel Korlinski who became a teacher and then head of the yeshiva Tifferet Zvi in Jerusalem; and Mikka Finkel. A few students also came from the Merkaz Harav [yeshiva] in Jerusalem, including: Zvi Neria, who became the head of Yeshiva Kfar Haroeh and founder of Bnei Akiva yeshivas; and Dov Raffel, who became an educator and researcher in the field of education, and a professor at Bar Ilan University.

One of our meeting places was in the Weissman furniture carpentry shop in Tel Arza. That's where they dis-

---

Golde. She is a healer. She might be able to help your daughter." The woman made her way to the Bubbe's clinic. When she got there she was astonished to see the woman she had met at the kotel. "Why didn't you tell me who you were?" she asked. "If I just told you that I was a healer you wouldn't believe me," she answered. "This way you came with a recommendation." And, of course, she was able to help the young woman recover.

75 Three members of the Japanese Red Army terrorist group had checked machine guns and grenades into their luggage and opened fire in the baggage area of Lod (now Ben Gurion) Airport. One terrorist survived and was sentenced to a life imprisonment in Israel. In 1985 he was part of a prisoner exchange and went to Lebanon, where he was eventually given asylum in 2000, in the face of an extradition request of the Japanese government. http://www.nytimes.com/2000/03/18/world/lebanon-grants-political-asylum-to-1-of-5-japan-terrorists.html?scp=13&sq=Lod%20Airport%20Massacre%201972&st=cse

tributed guns and we'd go out into the evening to guard in Sanhedria, Geulah and elsewhere. The sergeant who distributed the weapons was a constable with the rank of sergeant in the *Yishuv* policemen, a Polish immigrant, by the name of Chaim Tzudik [Zadok]. He later became Minister of Justice, Minister of Industry and Commerce, and Minister of Religion during the 60's and 70's.

One cold night in 1936 the Haganah commander ordered me and three others to hide by the Dung Gate in order to catch Arabs who used to throw rocks at Jews who were on their way to pray at the *Kotel*.[76] We lay down among the cactus plants waiting to catch the ruffians, but it was all for naught. That night nobody appeared. At three in the morning, frozen to the bone, we went into the Sephardic Porat Yosef synagogue to drink some tea.[77] Around ten Torah scholars sat there and learned. Even there I managed to hear praise of Abba. One of them pointed at me and said, "This is the son of Rabbi Frank." One Jew approached me and said: "You are so fortunate! Your father is the greatest rabbi. I've participated in meetings with rabbis and judges, all of them talking and arguing. Your father was the only one who waited quietly until they turned to him. And then everyone got quiet, and in a few short sentences he laid out the question that had arisen and suggested his solution. And instantly all the drivel and chatter collapsed like a house of cards."

We occasionally returned to Kiriat Anavim for training or guard duty—sometimes with one of the high ranking

---

76 The Dung Gate is the entrance to the Old City of Jerusalem that is closest to the Kotel. It got its name from the fact that it was a primary location for garbage dumping from the time of the temple through the 19th century.
77 This yeshiva, located not far from the *kotel*, the largest and most important of the sephardic yeshivot in the city wasn't built until 1923, but the land was purchased in 1909, financed by Yosef Shalom, a Jewish merchant and philanthropist in Calcutta, India. Ben Arieh Vol. I, p. 414.

commanders of the Haganah and the first commander of the Palmach (the Haganah elite strike force), Yitzchak Sadeh, whom everyone called "the old man."[78] Once Yitzchak Sadeh even went out with us on night maneuvers.

We were young, and so we were still prone to mischief. One time we got the kibbutz goat drunk with arak. The drunken goat went into the dining hall while it was being prepared for a meal. A few of the young women fled outside screaming: "He's haunted by a *dybbuk*!" (demon)

EVERY YEAR I WAITED IMPATIENTLY TO CELEBRATE SIMchat Torah. The flow of visitors to Abba's sukkah never ceased during the holiday. This one came to learn some Torah, this one came to bless him, another would come to taste Imma's baked goods, and all of them filled with a joyous mood as it is written: "And you shall rejoice on your holidays." On Simchat Torah it was the custom that the worshippers would come to our house to accompany Abba to the synagogue with singing and dancing.[79] I would greet those who came with a light drink and the impressive parade would head out. However, in 1938, right before the holiday began, I received a summons from the Haganah to go to Yehezkel Street next to the Tnuva (dairy and chicken cooperative) Building. I told Abba sadly that I'd be unable to accompany him to the synagogue along with everyone else.

---

78 "Sadeh was a memorable character, a powerfully built, ebullient bull of a man, a veteran of the Red Army and a committed Marxist. He infused his own self-confidence and reckless exuberance into his young officers. These included such teenagers as Yigal Peicovitch (later Allon) and Moshe Dayan, both of whom eventually would play vital roles in the emergent army and government of Israel." Sachar, p .214.
79 I remember my mother's description of this tradition, how moving and impressive it was to see hundreds of people gathering and singing, "*Va-yehi b'yeshurun melech* ..." "There was a king in Jerusalem ..."

Abba didn't object. He always thought that being Jewish also meant protecting the Jewish people. "An order's an order," he said, "let the Holy One protect all of you." Imma looked worried, but didn't say a word.

Fifteen young men gathered next to the Tnuva Building. We boarded a truck and headed out towards Kiriat Anavim. We were told that Arabs in the village of Saris (today's Shoresh) were shooting at the road to Jerusalem. We were given weapons, spread out in the sector and hid among the rocks in the area where Kiriat Telz-Stone stands today. Towards evening a British airplane came and fired some warning shots at the village of Saris. Despite this, there were a few shots fired from the village, but afterwards it was quiet. No one was injured and we didn't return fire—in part so as not to reveal ourselves and in part to conserve ammunition. We lay hidden by the rocks all night long.

I thought of the Simchat Torah celebrations that I was missing in the synagogue with mixed feelings. On one hand, I was regretful, but on the other hand I knew that because of our actions the worshippers would be able to enjoy the holiday in peace. At daybreak we were told to return to Kiriat Anavim, but then we learned that the Arabs had rolled large boulders to block the road. Again we were delayed until a British police force came and opened the road. I didn't get back to Jerusalem until the holiday was over.

In the Haganah we were ten men to a group. We came from different traditions and had different points of view, but this didn't get in the way of creating long lasting friendships. There was fellowship between the religious and the secular and mutual respect. We loved one another and were devoted to one another. When a secular Haganah member needed to bring a message to a religious member, he would put on a *kippa* before he entered the house. Completely secular people were sensitive to the feelings of the religious and were considerate to them. The religious participated in the secular experience and, when necessary, went out on actions on Shabbat or yom tov, still wrapped in a tallit.

Nowadays both sides have become more extreme and I blame parties on both sides of the divide that fan the flames of enmity and destroy the sense of national unity. If we could only lower the intensity of extremism on both sides our national condition would be improved. A nation without faith can't endure, and faith without a nation is a return to exile. These mutual needs were well understood by the Jews of *Eretz Yisrael* in that era, before we had a state of our own.

THE LEADERSHIP OF THE *YISHUV* ENCOURAGED THE youth to enlist in the Mandate Police in order to increase the number of Jewish guardians. I responded to this call and joined a guard course (*Gefirim*, as they were called) in the police training academy on Mt. Scopus in Jerusalem.[80] The academy was run by the British, and both Jews and Arabs enlisted there. Ironically the leader of our section was an Arab sergeant who wanted to demonstrate his mastery of the Hebrew language. He ordered us in simple and understandable language: "I am a whistle—you are columns—two rows!" We restrained our snickers only with great difficulty. Someone whispered, trying not to shriek with laughter,

---

80 There were "3,000 authorized *"ghaffirs,"* uniformed Jewish auxiliary guards (whose parallel membership in the Haganah the British accepted). Even more significantly, the man appointed by the British as operating commander of the *ghaffirs*, Captain Orde Wingate, vigorously and imaginatively enlarged Sadeh's concept of 'active defense.'" Sachar, p. 215. See below for more about Wingate.

"The sergeant means that the minute he blows the whistle we have to organize into two lines." By the way, the salary due me for my services, nine and half *agorot*, has yet to be paid. From time to time my good mother used to give me a few *grosh* for pocket money.

The tensions between Jews and Arabs didn't subside within the police academy. In 1937, when a group of scouts left a performance in the Edison Theater in Jerusalem an Arab sniper shot at them and killed three young Jewish men. The murderer managed to disappear in a getaway car that whisked him away, just like terrorist acts today. The next day at the academy one of my friends, Ya'akov Lampert, heard an Arab say to his buddy, "Last night we took out three of them." Lampert turned around and gave the Arab a punch in face and broke a few teeth. (Lampert's brother, Yehudah, was a member of Etzel who died during the War of Independence near Ramle). *[Note by Avraham Frank: Yaakov Lampert had three brothers. They lived at 29 Yochanan HaSandlar in Tel Aviv. While he himself was a policeman and had permission to carry a pistol, his brother Yehudah Lamfert (b.1925) was a member of Etzel, who achieved a rank of platoon commander, known as Avidan. In the winter of 1948 Yehudah and his platoon guarded an area on the border of Jaffa and joined in the attack on the Manashia neighborhood in northern Jaffa. In this battle they lost the majority of their soldiers. Within two weeks Yehudah managed to regroup and form his platoon anew and joined Etzel's attack on Ramle immediately after the state was declared and he fell there (5/20/1948) in a battle at the entrance to the city. He was brought to his eternal rest in the military cemetery in Kiryat Shaul (from the memorial volume published by the ministry of defense)]*

When I was a student in the Gafrir course at the police training school on Mr. Scopus, Jerusalem 1937

In 1938 the Haganah sent me and another two Jerusalemites to a training course in [Kibbutz] Ein Harod. I'll never forget the opening ceremony: we wore uniforms, stood at strict attention and the great Orde Wingate[81] himself appeared and declared in British accented Hebrew: " I am

---

81 Wingate was a British captain who strongly supported the return of Jews to their land, even though he himself was not Jewish. He worked closely with the Haganah and helped develop their training and tactics. Yitzchak Sadeh was a student and close associate. According to Moshe Dayan, before beginning any military action he would read a passage in the Bible which testified to the victory of God and the Jews. Gilbert, p.93. Wingate developed "Special Night Squads," which were more aggressive than Sadeh's tactics, conducting audacious surprise raids against guerilla hideouts. Wingate's pro-Zionist views became an embarrassment to the British government and in the spring of 1939 he was sent back to England. Sachar, p. 215-16.

pleased to found the first Zionist army in the land of Israel." After this he continued in English. He spoke of the establishment of night patrols, and the department for guarding the gas pipeline that led from Iraq to Haifa, which was under constant attack by Arab gangs. He concluded his address by emphasizing that we'd be learning in three weeks what a British trainee would learn in three months, but during that time we'd chit chat as much as a British soldier would in a year. Even though Orde Wingate was a staunch supporter of the Zionist enterprise, he quickly learned the ways of Jewish enlistees and had a hard time accepting their weak point—that they were inveterate chatterers.

Orde Wingate, called "The Friend" by the Jewish *Yishuv*, based his military doctrine on small unit commando tactics which included: Initiative, sophistication, flexibility and night maneuvers. All of these actors influenced the practices of the Palmach and Tzahal (Israel Defense Force) from the very outset.

As we drew near to the end of the course there was talk that our unit would be sent to the Suez Canal in order to strengthen the forces that were stationed there in case the German army attempted to invade Israel from there (as occurred in 1942, when the German army tried to invade Eretz Yisrael by way of Egypt, and was stopped by the British army in el-Alamein, west of Alexandria). However, in late September, 1938, the Munich Conference ended. Lord Chamberlain, the prime minister of Britain, returned home and announced that he had "brought peace in our times" and waved the piece of paper signed by Hitler. That was before we knew that the agreement would become a symbol of humiliating British submission to German aggression and the war's outbreak was only delayed by one year.

Night raiding course of Wingate. I am the second from the left, with my Haganah buddies. Ein Harod 1938

In light of these developments, our mission was changed, and when the course at Ein Harod ended I was sent to Kibbutz Gan Shmuel. Our commander, Ya'akov Dubnow, put me on night patrol, with a permanent base in Kibbutz Mishmarot.[82] We conducted night patrols on foot in the area of Givat Edah, Wadi Arah and Shafiya. The greatest threat to the population came from the leaders of two bands of brigands: Abu Dura and Abu Jilda. The name "Abu Jilda" took on a mythical meaning. Mothers would warn their children, "If you don't finish this food, Abu Jilda will come and kidnap you!"

I returned to Jerusalem three months later, towards the end of 1938. In May, 1939, the British published their "White Paper," in which the British government proclaimed

---

[82] The kibbutz is located east of Ceasarea, on would have been close to the 1948 armistice lines.

its position regarding the Israel question.[83] Severe restrictions were placed on immigration, and real estate sales to Jews were forbidden in most of the land. This collection of harsh enactments unleashed a wave of protests and actions on the part of the *Yishuv* and the Zionist movement throughout the world. The *Yishuv*, despite all its internal divisions, rose up against the British government, assisted "illegal" immigrants and took a more extremist response towards the British. Meanwhile, the Arab gangs continued to attack the *Yishuv*. Throughout the land Jews went out to defend themselves. A giant demonstration was held in Jerusalem that spread all the way from the Zion Theater on Jaffa Road to the "Generali" building. From noon until nighttime we clashed and fought with the English police and they responded mercilessly with their clubs.[84]

At ten o'clock that night I stood among the angry crowd along with three Haganah friends: Zvi Spektor, Avraham Nuriel, and Yitzchak Hecker. (All three of them were lost in the tragic "23 sailors [incident]," when 23 Haganah

---

[83] The White Paper was issued by colonial secretary, Malcolm McDonald, in May, 1939. Although it was unacceptable to both Arabs and Jews, Zionists were especially enraged, given the Nazi threat to the survival of the Jewish people. The Jewish Agency declared "It is in the darkest hour of Jewish history that the British Government proposes to deprive the Jews of their last hope, and to close the road back to their Homeland." Tessler, p.245-46. When World War II broke out only months later, David Ben Gurion famously declared, "We will fight with the British against Hitler as if there were no White Paper; we will fight the White Paper as if there were no war." Gilbert. P.101

[84] The May 18, 1939 edition of the New York Times described "terrific battles" between the police and Jewish youth protesting Britain's new policies. "After the Jews had made an orderly demonstration march through the central streets of the city, about 5,000 Jewish youth assembled in the early afternoon in front of the district Commissioner's office to carry on their protest against Britain's policy. Booing the police and throwing stones, they drew a baton charge by the police. The crowd recoiled somewhat, then pressed forward, hurling stones ... Then wave after wave of policemen charged down Jaffa Road with batons swinging here and there. The Jewish youth, refusing to give way, replied with stones or any objects they could seize. For three hours the battle continued without a let up." The paper reports that one British policeman died, and 135 demonstrators were wounded, many of them seriously. http://query.nytimes.com/mem/archive/pdf?res=F1091FFD3C54107A93CBA8178ED85F4D8385F9

men set out by boat, May 18, 1941, to conduct sabotage in Tripoli, Lebanon. They never returned and their fate remains a mystery). Somebody near us shot and killed an English soldier and wounded three others. The elite Scottish Black Watch unit appeared on the streets, and we heard shots. Many people were wounded and we were busy taking them to safety. Imma immediately laundered my clothing in order to remove any evidence that I had been present at the upheaval. The next morning Shmulke, an undercover British policeman came to the house. He warned Imma: "The English know about your son. He's got to get out of here fast!" Imma immediately sent me to my sister Rachel in Tel Aviv. I followed her orders and left Jerusalem and went to live with my sister. This Shmulke lived on David Yellin Street in the Zichron Moshe neighborhood. Two weeks before the State was declared he was shot and killed in his home by two young men—I don't know if they were members of Etzel or of Lechi (two militant groups).

My sister's husband, Yisrael Kaplan, built the first spring factory in Israel and offered me a job working for him. The factory produced springs for mattresses and springs for British army vehicles, but secretly we also produced springs for guns, pistols, grenades and landmines for the Haganah and Etzel.[85] The workers themselves thought that we were making springs for jack-in-the-box toys, but actually they were springs for Sten machine guns. One day some British policemen came by and saw the rings we had made that would be inserted to lock grenades (which were called Menachem B.). They asked, "What are these rings for?"

---

85 Etzel is the acronym for Irgun Tzeva Leumi (sometimes called "Irgun" for short), a militant underground group led by Menachem Begin after 1944. Inspired by Zev Jabotinsky, they called for more direct and violent actions against Arabs and the British. They did not accept the authority of the Jewish Agency

Without batting an eyelash I answered: "Oh, those are for window blinds."

When World War II broke out there was a shortage of raw materials. You couldn't get steel and iron filaments to make springs. I discovered that tires contained iron threads in their sidewalls, so I went to Gaza and bought surplus tires from the British army. Back at the factory in Tel Aviv we separated out the iron threads from the tires and we used it to make springs for the Haganah Sten guns and Etzel grenades.

IN 1940 I RETURNED TO JERUSALEM SO I COULD CELebrate Rosh Hashanah at home with my parents. The day after the holiday I went to the Egged (bus) station on Jaffa Road to go back to Tel Aviv. Right before I got on the bus, at 10:30 in the morning, I remembered that I had forgotten to say goodbye to Imma, so I called to tell her that I was leaving for Tel Aviv. She asked me to delay my trip. "We don't have any kerosene at home. Go to Meah Shearim and get us a can of kerosene before you leave." I did so, and was back at the Egged by noon. The bus left, but shortly thereafter we got stuck in a big traffic jam. It turned out that the 10:30 bus had been involved in a terrible accident, and was hit by a train while crossing the tracks near Ramle. The train dragged the bus about 100 meters, burst into flames and the passengers were burned alive. In those days the bus windows were covered with bars in order to thwart the various schemes of Arab gangs along the roads. So when the fire broke out the passengers were trapped inside. My life was spared because of Imma's request.

An Egged armored bus in the days of the British Mandate

"Shmuel," a Lechi Man

The fact that I was a Haganah member didn't prevent me from becoming friends with members of Lechi,[86] a rival underground group. One of my best friends, Yosef ben David, lived in the settlement of Nachalat Yehudah, near Rishon Le'Tziyon and was one of the founders of the organization. He was arrested by the British in 1941. He was incarcerated first in Latrun and was then transferred to Eritrea,[87] returning to Israel about six years after the State was declared. We remained in close friendly contact. Sadly, he died prematurely.

---

86 Lechi, an acronym of Lohamei Herut Yisrael, also known as the Stern Group [so named from its leader, Abraham Stern], seceded from Etzel and was considered to be more extreme than its parent organization. Tessler, p.207.

87 On October 19, 1944 the British authorities transferred 251 detainees to the Sambel prison camp in Asmara, Eritrea. By the end of the British mandate, 439 people were held there. After several escape attempts, the prisoners were transferred to the Sudan, then back to Eritrea and then to Kenya. Successful escapes were the trigger for the moves. The last of the prisoners arrived in Israel on July 12, 1948. http://www.etzel.org.il/english/ac15.htm

In the 1940's I became friendly with another Lechi member, Yehudah Levi, whose family had come to Israel from Italy. His underground name within Lechi was "Shmuel." He was regarded as having golden hands, and reached a high rank in the technical division of Lechi. He would frequently ask us for springs for weapons and we always provided them. Sometimes he'd encourage me to join Lechi and I always answered: "If I'm going to die, it'll only be within the ranks of the Haganah."

One cold day, around 1947, at the height of the War of Independence, Yehudah Levi appeared at my factory. I was happy to see him and surprised when he told me that he had reached the conclusion that a large military group was preferable to small underground groups. He asked if I would help him join the Haganah. I promised that I'd help and called the office of Yisrael Galili, one of the high ranking Haganah members. They sent one of their men, who sat and talked with him in the factory for a long time. After the investigation the Haganah man told me quietly: "A wonderful young man who has a great deal of knowledge." The two of them separated, but the Haganah men delayed their answer.

Every day towards evening Yehudah Levi would come to my factory and ask: "Nu? Any answer?" I'd have to apologize and let him know that the Haganah men hadn't yet responded. I worried about how the Lechi people would react and one wintry evening in January, 1948 I said to him: "Yehudah, you're in danger. Come stay at my house in Petach Tikva." He dismissed my offer, "Don't worry, nothing is going to happen to me. I carry a grenade in my belt on my right side and a weapon on the left."

That night his good friend from Lechi asked him for help in checking out a storehouse of ammunition in Raanana, and then shot him in the head. The next day I went to work and was horrified to see a death notice posted at the bus station: "Commander Shmuel fell in the line of duty." They used his nom de guerre.[88]

I immediately got in touch with my Haganah friends: "They terminated the young man," I said, my heart breaking in shock, grief and anger. The Haganah men went to search for him. They found him deposited at the site of the murder in Ranaana, and brought him for burial in the Nachalat Yitzchak cemetery. Later I learned that the order to liquidate "Shmuel" was given by Natan Yellin-Mor, the commander of Lechi[89].

Years later, in 1977, Yehudah Levi's brothers got in touch with me, wanting more details about our acquaintanceship and the last night of his life, when I suggested he stay with me in Petach Tikva and he refused. They told me that their father, who was at that time 101 years old, lived in an old age home. Two months later they invited me to a ceremony that was conducted in the old age home, where his son would be recognized as one of the fallen of the underground. The elderly father received the Alah decoration, the sign of Lechi members, and the father was recognized as one of the bereaved of Israel's battles.

---

[88] It would be hard to overstate the level of rancor-bordering-on-enmity that existed between the Haganah and the Etzel/Lechi groups. Their philosophies were dramatically divergent with disputes not only about responses to the British presence in Eretz Yisrael, but fundamental political differences; the Haganah was labor and socialist oriented, whereas Etzel was strongly opposed to socialism. There were serious misunderstandings on both sides and mutual mistrust. The personal animosity between David Ben Gurion on the Haganah side and Menachem Begin from Etzel persisted as long as the two lived.

[89] Natan Yellin-Mor (Friedman) was one of the founders of Lehi. Arrested by the British, he escaped from the prison camp in Latrun in 1943. He was charged in the murder of Count Folke Bernadotte, the United Nations mediator, in the fall of 1948, but the case against him could not be proven. Elected to the Israeli knesset in 1949 he underwent an ideological shift and became very left wing in his outlook, supporting a Jewish Arab federation in Palestine. He died in 1980. Encyclopedia Judaica in http://www.jewishvirtuallibrary.org/jsource/judaica/ejud_0002_0021_0_21240.html

This was not the only case I knew where Lechi had conducted a liquidation operation. One day with my own eyes I saw Eliyahu ben Tzuri liquidate a Jewish informer by the name of Fidler. This Fidler used to inform the British about young men who would post proclamations.[90] Lechi had warned Fidler several times, and when he didn't stop, it appears that they decided to kill him. Malkah and I were taking a walk on Allenby Road. She was pregnant with our daughter, Gitti. Suddenly, right across from Balfour Street I saw ben Tzuri standing at the corner, looking towards Fidler. "Come on! Let's get out of here! Something's about to happen," I said to Malkah. We got as far as the Great Synagogue on Allenby Road when we heard three shots ring out. "They liquidated him," I said to Malkah and she grabbed my hand so I wouldn't go back to check out the murder scene. A few months later, in November 1944 in Cairo, Eliyahu ben Tzuri and his friend Eliyahu Chakim attempted to assassinate Lord Bevin, the British Minister for Middle Eastern Affairs and an avowed anti-Semite. They were caught, tried and condemned to death by hanging.[91]

In the Haganah informers were punished, but they were never given a death sentence as was done in Etzel and Lechi. Two Haganah friends came to me in 1937, Moshe ben Giat and Mishka Rabinowitz, and told me that they had received an order to "take care of" an engineer in Jerusalem. He was a Jew, about 35 years old, who worked at the radio station of

---

90 In Israel, to this day it is customary to glue proclamations onto walls and billboards. They could be advertisements for events, death announcements, or calls to action.

91 The assassination was actually of Lord Moyne (Walter Guinness), the new British Minister-Resident in Cairo, on November 4, 1944. Eliahu Hakim and Eliahu Ben Tsouri were tried and then executed on March 22, 1945. This assassination by two members of Lechi provoked great outrage among the British people and parliament, as well as the Jewish Agency Executive. It also led to the "saison," the period during which the Jewish Agency handed over 700 Irgun names to the British authorities, most of whom were then arrested. Gilbert, pp.118-19.

the British Mandate. One day he insisted that the Haganah clear out the weapons that were hidden in the building where he lived. He threatened that if they didn't comply, he would reveal the secret to the British. These two fellows had followed him for two days, but since his home was behind the Battei Hungarim in Jerusalem, and close to the British police station, they feared being caught and came to me. The three of us went out, followed him a few hours, and eventually cornered him on Nevi'im Street near Hadassah. We "tuned him up," and two days later he came to the Haganah commander and announced: "It's okay, the cache can stay where it is."

Most of the small Jewish population of the *Yishuv*, which, when all was said and done, numbered fewer than 600,000 souls, considered themselves as part of the struggle against the British. Malkah's mother, Rachel, a wonderful woman, once saw two young men running away while British soldiers chased them, handguns drawn. The young men had, apparently, posted placards on the street near her house in Jerusalem. Even though she had never identified herself with the underground movements, and certainly wasn't active in the fight against the British, she gestured towards them to come to her house and she hid them under some beds. When the British soldiers came near she invited them to come in, told her daughters to pour coffee for them and warmly hosted them. They had no suspicions about anything, thanked her for the hospitality and left. After they had gone a distance she told the boys, "Okay. The coast is clear, go in peace."

IN 1945 A HAGANAH MAN BY THE NAME OF YAAKOV Zakai came to see me. His father, David Zakai, was active in the Eretz Yisrael Workers Party (*Mapai*), and was a journalist at the daily paper for the general workers organization, *Davar*, where he wrote for decades, and, for a time, served as its editor. Yaakov Zakai told me about Jewish inmates incarcerated in the Jerusalem jail who were being beaten by Arab inmates.

"I want to smuggle in some kind of weapon so that they can protect themselves," he said.

"I can come up with something," I promised him, "but I have no idea how you could sneak it into the jail."

"Don't worry. You make it, and I'll find a way to pass it along to the prisoners."

I created a weapon that was called in the German translation, *"makat mavet."* (fatal blow) I threaded three springs one inside the other, at a length of about 12 cm. each, small enough to hide in your pocket. When you use the device the three springs come out one after the other, as if through a telescope, and creating a whip about 30 cm. long. You wouldn't want to be the guy on the receiving end of this spring.

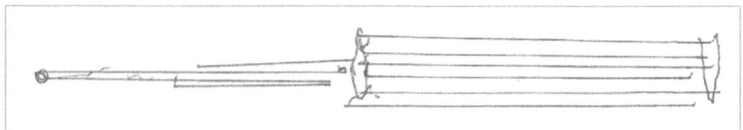

An improvised weapon for the captive underground fighters, drawn by memory 60 years after its invention

I made five of these devices and gave them to Yaakov. About a month later I ran into him and he said just one sentence: "Avraham, you did excellent work."

In July 1947, when my daughter Gitti was about one and a half years old, we went to visit my Uncle Tanchum in Chadera. Around that time Etzel kidnapped two British sergeants in an attempt to prevent the hanging of three Etzel members, Avshalom Haviv, Meir Necker and Yaakov Weiss, who had been sentenced to death. The British responded by imposing a curfew on Netanya and the entire area. The British searched for the kidnapped sergeants for three weeks, conducting house to house searches. On July 29, 1947, ignoring the pleas of the Yishuv leaders, and many people throughout the world, and despite the warnings of Etzel, the three Etzel members were taken by the British to the gallows. In response, the two British sergeants were hung. Their bodies were found the next day hanging in a grove near Netanya which is, to this day, called "Sergeant's Grove."[92]

I didn't want to stay in Chadera with my wife and daughter when the British were in a retaliatory mood, so I decided that we'd go to Haifa. On Jaffa Road in Haifa, next to Barclays Bank, there were three young men whom I recognized as members of Lechi and I sensed that even Haifa wouldn't be quiet. I told Malkah that we had to leave quickly. We wanted to go to Tiberias, but the only bus available went to Safed. "So we'll go to Safed," I said and we headed north to get away from the anticipated arrests by the British. We stayed in Safed for three days, and afterwards we went to Jerusalem and we stayed with Malkah's parents in Jerusalem.

A few days later, August 6, 1947, we were walking along Neviim Street with little Gitti in her stroller. Suddenly we heard an explosion and it turned out that Etzel saboteurs had blown up the government labor office on Neviim Street, which served the British. Our little baby burst into tears. We hugged her close while all around us stunned people ran

---

92 Not only were the sergeants executed, but the ground beneath them was booby-trapped, to injure those who would remove the bodies. This act increased the pressure on the part of the British public to bring home British soldiers stationed in Palestine. Gilbert, p.149

to the area of the explosion. I worried about my family. In order to protect them and find a quiet and secure place we had left Hadera, and then Haifa, Safed and then to Jerusalem. And now it became clear that the entire land was in flames; the struggle against the British and the Arabs was still at its height with no end in sight.

Chapter Four

Malkah Joins

THE VOICE OF THE BRIDEGROOM AND THE VOICE OF THE BRIDE
(FROM ONE OF THE WEDDING BLESSINGS)

Avraham

I was 26 years old, certainly of an age where it was customary to talk about marriage, but I couldn't find a woman after my own heart. My mother wasn't happy that her son was living the bachelor life in Tel Aviv, and pressed me to get married. During that time my mother became gravely ill. She suffered from pneumonia which got worse and worse. During one of my visits to Jerusalem, and probably because she didn't completely trust me, my mother made me swear with a handshake that I wouldn't propose marriage to anyone before inviting her to the house and getting my parent's blessing to the match. I promised her that I would do as she said, but before the week was out, in 1943, when she was only 66 years old, my mother died. Before she departed, she said to my sister, "If Avraham finds his intended he should get married right away, and not wait for the end of the year of mourning." Abba, in his own inimitable way, also told me, "When people speak with you about matches, you must listen. If your heart isn't in it, you don't have to agree to the match, but you must listen."

With my beloved on our wedding day.

I had not yet met Malkah before my mother died. Maybe I had seen her once or twice during my youth in Jerusalem in 1935, as I described earlier, when I came to her house to get posters for distribution. But in those days she stayed on the outskirts, overshadowed by her brothers and sisters, and I didn't really notice her. Malkah's father, Rabbi Yitzchak Jaffe, and her brother Leibel, I knew well. I knew Leibel from childhood, and when we grew older we had a "business" relationship. Her brother acquired weapons and ammunitions from many different "private" sources and I would buy them from him and turn them over to the Haganah. One day I came home and Abba said to me, "Leibel, Reb Yitzchak's son, is looking for you." "I'll see him when I go back to Tel Aviv," I promised. I went to Tel Aviv, and came to Leibel's apartment on Maccabbi Street, near King George Street. He showed me a German revolver, a "Parabelus." I didn't want to know when or how he got it, and asked for no details. I made a quick decision and bought it for the Haganah for six lira.

While we were talking, a wonderful young woman came into the room. "What a lovely guest you have," I said to Leibel. He said, "That's my sister." "So lovely and from my home town," I thought to myself and hinted to Leibel that I was interested in meeting her. The truth is, I was deeply regretting that I had already committed myself to a meeting with my Haganah friends later that day.

I was surprised that we hadn't met previously, but I felt as if I had known her for a very long time, since our families were in such close contact and we lived not far away from one another. That week I had weapons training on Sunday and Monday. So I asked her if I could visit on Tuesday and she agreed. To my great fortune the Monday class was cancelled and I went immediately to her brother's house, I knocked on the door and asked, "Could I visit you already today?" Malkah laughed and invited me in.

We didn't go to the movies because I was mourning my mother. We walked along the beach, drank sodas and we conversed, but, faithful to my promise, I wanted to get Abba's agreement and permission before I proposed to her. The next day I got in touch with Abba and told him that I had met the daughter of Reb Yitzchak and that I liked her very much. That same week, on Thursday afternoon, one of my brothers-in-law came to the factory in Tel Aviv and gave me a letter from Abba. In the letter he wrote: "I invited Reb Yitzchak to talk things over and he told me that he has no objections."

The only thing left to do was to ask the young woman herself! That evening I met with Malkah. We went to "London Square" continuing down to the beach and said I said to her, "I'm a busy man and I don't like to waste time. I know your father from childhood, he knows me, so let's get married!"

"But I don't know you," she answered, and justifiably so, since it had only been four days since we first met.

"You'll get to know me as time goes on. A couple can live together for ten years and not know one another," I said.

"But I'm still young," she responded logically.

"So you'll grow old together with me," I said.

The acquaintanceship between us was so brief that when Malkah went to Jerusalem for Shabbat she was unable to even describe my appearance to her family. My sister Esther suggested that I also come to Jerusalem and on Saturday night we'd sign the *tena'im* (betrothal agreement). I caught the last bus to Jerusalem on Friday and Abba told me that Malkah's brother-in-law, Nechemia Marek, the husband of Malkah's oldest sister, would come to *daven* in the synagogue and that he would let Malkah's father know that I had arrived. As planned, on Saturday night Malkah's family came to us, the fathers signed the *tena'im* and we were engaged.

Malkah

For the first time in my life they sewed me a new dress. Until the wedding I always got hand-me-downs from my older sisters.

Our wedding was on 4/4/44, during the height of Second World War. The only guests were brothers and sisters. The wedding was held in the Frank house in Jerusalem at noon, because there was a British curfew at night.

Avraham

My father was quite happy with the betrothal. He had great respect for the Jaffe family and saw that I had found a woman faithful to the tradition, wise and good hearted. He knew that she would create a warm Jewish home and that's exactly what happened. There was never a Shabbat when we didn't host friends of the family, and sometimes a random tourist whom I brought home from the synagogue, and everyone was impressed with the warm hospitality and Malkah's culinary skill. She never complained about my long hours at work, the small salary I drew, or that she raised the children practically by herself. Over time we learned to complement and compromise with one another, with patience and peacefulness.

With Abba.

On the first Rosh Hashanah after our wedding we came to "do" the holiday with Malkah's parents. There were other brothers-in-law and they all went to *Tashlich* by the cistern in front of the house. I didn't go with them and Malkah's mother said to her husband, "This 'treasure' didn't recite *Tashlich*."[93]

Reb Yitzchak Jaffe asked me, "Why didn't you recite *Tashlich*?"

---

93 Many Jews have a custom to go to a water source, usually a river or spring, on the first day of Rosh Hashanah and symbolically cast ones sins away. Jerusalem has no river and only one spring, the Shiloah near the Old City, so a cistern would have to do.

"My father doesn't recite *Tashlich*, so I am also exempt," I answered.

"First learn to study like your father, and then you can act as he does," Malkah's father scolded me.

The next day we went to Abba's house and I recited the *kiddush* over arak[94] instead of wine."

"What's this??" my father asked.

"My *shver* (father-in-law) recites *kiddush* over arak, so I do the same."

"First learn to study like your *shver*, and then you can do *kiddush* as he does," Abba said.

Malkah and I looked at one another and smiled. There was mutual respect and honor between the two families, and this is but one example among many.

Malkah

After the wedding we looked for an apartment in Tel Aviv. At that time it was difficult to find rooms in the city. First we lived in a laundry room on the roof of an apartment house on Ha-Chashmal Street, next to Moshavot Square in Tel Aviv. The bathroom facilities were on the other side of the roof and a large tub stood in the "apartment". None of this prevented us from hosting friends and family. That's where we brought home Gitti, who was born in 1945 in the private hospital of Dr. Sodovski in Jerusalem. After a year and a half we moved to Mohaliver Street in Petach Tikva. We rented a two room apartment with a small garden and a leaky roof, and our circumstances were much better than our rooftop apartment in Tel Aviv. That's where our two sons were born, Yigal in 1949 and Raffi in 1952.

---

94 An anise based high proof liquor popular in the middle east.

The Jaffe Family, My Wife's Family

Avraham

Malkah's father, Rabbi Yitzchak Jaffe, who was a teacher and a rabbinic court representative, often consulted with my father. But I never knew his daughter and it is strange that we never met even though we were born in Jerusalem and lived not far away from each other.

Malkah

My father greatly respected Rav Frank. Every day he would go to the Frank home, and felt quite at home there. He also loved to converse with Avraham's mother, who was a wise and practical woman, who had both feet rooted in the ground.

My grandmother's mother, Tamar Lubin, was eight years old when a powerful earthquake hit Safed in 1837.[95] Her parents perished and she was plucked out from the ruins safe and sound. She later became a midwife and she was known as "the midwife of Safed." Her daughter, my grandmother, Yocheved Kannel, grew up and married in Safed, and gave birth to my mother there.

In 1888, when my mother, Rachel, was three months old, the young family moved to Jerusalem. A few years later they moved to Shechem (Nablus), and my mother well remembered her nursery school there, which included both Jewish and Arab children. The settlers left for Jerusalem six months later, and that's where my mother lived until her death.

---

95 The 1837 earthquake caused enormous destruction; 4,000 Jews died in the devastation. Scientists have estimated that the magnitude range was 6.25-6.8, centered in the Jordan Rift Valley, traditionally an area with significant seismic activity. Through the philanthropy of an Italian Jewish scholar, Rav Yitzchak Goyatos, the Jewish quarter was rebuilt, with most of the reconstruction completed by 1847. http://www.safed.co.il/safed-earthquakes.html

The Jaffe family during the exile to Damascus, Jerusalem 1917.

Malka sitting on her mother's lap, Jerusalem circa 1928.

Rabbi Yitzchak Jaffe's family seems to have emigrated from Poland, since they lived in the "Warsaw Kollel." Abba's first wife died, leaving him with five young orphans. He married Imma in 1910. This was also her second marriage. Her first husband had tuberculosis and died shortly after their wedding, while she was in early pregnancy with her first born son, Channaniah, named for his departed father, Channaniah Davis. Imma was young and beautiful, 22 years old, and Abba adopted her infant son.

During World War I, when there was a severe famine in Jerusalem, Imma sent her oldest son, Channaniah, to the Diskin Orphan's Home.[96] There he at least had food. The situation was so dire that people scavenged through the garbage searching for peelings from fruits or vegetables. Imma sold blankets and beds to the Circassians for a little bread.[97] She, my father and seven of their children were deported to Damascus, while two children remained in Jerusalem. After the war additional children were born in Jerusalem, including me.

My father's first born from his first marriage, Moshe Jaffe, was 16 years old when his father married my mother, and he decided to leave Jerusalem. Apparently, he found it difficult to come to terms with his father's second marriage to the young and beautiful woman. He went to Jaffa and sailed off to England. He had a hard time making a living in England, serving as a temporary cantor in different places. In 1912 he managed to get a job as a furnace stoker on the

---

96 The orphanage was founded in 1881 by Rabbi Yehoshua Leib Diskin. Missionary societies targeted Jewish orphans, and offered them food and a home. Rabbi Diskin began the orphanage in his home and then it was expanded into an institution that still serves underprivileged children today. Tidhar, p. 565-66.
97 The Circassians are a Christian ethnic group, originally from the Caucasus Mountain region of Russia. After the Russian invasion of their homeland, many survivors made their way to the Balkans and then to the middle east in the 1880's. Circassianworld.com

new luxury liner "Titanic," that was ready for its maiden voyage to the United States. On the 10th of April, 1912, the Titanic left from the port of Southampton to New York. As a luxury ship (a first class ticket cost the equivalent of $50,000 in 2006 dollars), the Titanic had elevators, a swimming pool, a squash court and gym. The captain gave a speech before the thousands of people sailing and said, roughly speaking: "This ship was built to such modern standards and quality that no power in the world can damage it." Four days later, on the 14th of April, the ship was hit by an iceberg in the North Atlantic. The iceberg split the buoyancy compartments of the ship and just three hours later it sank. One thousand five hundred and thirteen of the 2,200 passengers drowned in the Atlantic Ocean. The children were rescued by the lifeboats. Moshe Jaffe, who was short and skinny and looked like a child, managed to board one of the lifeboats and was rescued. According to him, while the boat was rocking in the middle of the ocean, and the passengers scared to death, he remembered his father who feared that in America he might become an apostate. He swore that if he survived he would remain religious and carefully observe the *mitzvot*.[98]

Avraham

In 1957, when he was 62, Moshe returned to Israel to see his father. On Friday afternoon, half an hour before candle lighting, he appeared at our home in Tel Aviv. We were a young family and this was the first time we had met Malkah's brother from her father's first marriage. Moshe apologized for suddenly showing up without warning and

---

[98] I have looked through the names listed on the official Titanic website, and was unsuccessful in finding Moshe Jaffe, or a similar name.

said, "Abba told me that your house is always open, and whoever is in need is welcome." Truly, some people used to joke, saying "Why don't you put a sign on your door saying 'Frank Hotel'?"

Malkah

All together, my parents had 14 children. I was born in 1926, about 10 years after the deportation to Damascus. We lived with limited means, but were not impoverished. At the end of World War I, the men of the Warsaw Kollel turned to Abba and offered him the opportunity to run a pharmacy they had just founded. My father, who was a smart man and an autodidact, learned to read the Latin letters and pharmaceuticals and took the position after consulting with doctors.

When I was about 16 years old, my sister, Rivka, who was already married to Shmuel Eisenman, became ill. She suffered from fluid in her lungs and came to convalesce at our parents' home. At the same time my mother was ill with the flu. I cared for both of them and ran the house. One day my brother Leibel (Aryeh) came to visit from his home in Tel Aviv. He said that my mother and sister had improved and suggested that I come with him to rest up a few days at his home in Tel Aviv. Imma pounced on the idea and urged me to go with him. That's how Avraham and I happened to meet in Tel Aviv.

Chapter Five

Leaving Jerusalem

The War of Independence

On November 29, 1947 we were glued to the radio listening to the live broadcast of the meeting of the General Assembly of the United Nations regarding the partition of the land into two nations, Arab and Jewish. The Jewish people in Israel and around the world held their collective breath. Counting the votes of the various nations was accompanied by almost unbearable tension. At two in the morning the long hoped for announcement burst from the radio set. By a vote of 33 in favor, 13 opposed and 10 abstentions, the United Nations General Assembly decided to divide Palestine into two countries, Jewish and Arab. A wave of supreme elation flooded the small Jewish *Yishuv* and Jews throughout the world.[99]

---

99 My parents were living with Rav Frank on Malachi Street at that time and have told us about the immense euphoria that gripped the city and the country at that moment. In his memoir, Israeli novelist Amos Oz describes the moment when the final vote was tallied; he lived just blocks away from Malachi Street: " … our far-away street on the edge of Kerem Avraham in northern Jerusalem also roared all at once in a first terrifying shout that tore through the darkness and the buildings and trees, piercing itself, not a shout of joy, nothing like the shouts of spectators in sports grounds or excited rioting crowds, perhaps more like a scream of horror and bewilderment, a cataclysmic shout, a shout that could shift rocks, that could freeze your blood, as though all the dead who ever had died here and all those still to die had received a brief window to shout, and the next moment the scream of horror was replaced by roars of joy and a medley of hoarse cries …" Oz, Amos, *A Tale of Love and Darkness* translated by Nicholas de Lange, Harcourt Inc., 2004. p. 356.

We believed that this signaled a new era in the history of the Jewish people, but already the next day Jewish transportation was attacked near Petach Tikva, the road to Jerusalem was blockaded and the War of Independence broke out. I joined the Haganah forces guarding Petach Tikva. Many young men enlisted and some gave their lives defending Israel. There was a lot of black humor among the fighters, and we'd say to one another, "We have one general whose orders we always salute, and his name is 'there is no alternative.' [*ein brerah*]"

It's hard to believe, and there are many who try to suppress the memory, but from the small Jewish population in Eretz Yisrael, there were only about 23,000 in the fighting force, including inhabitants of various settlements who defended their homes armed only with light weapons. We had no tanks, artillery or warships, only a few light planes that were primarily used for communication missions. The local Arab population fought against us and they were joined by volunteers of a "rescue force," led by Colonel Fawzi al-Qawukji of Syria,[100] furnished with artillery and armored vehicles, a Druze battalion that also arrived from Syria and units from the regular forces of Arab nations: Jordan, Lebanon, Egypt, Iraq and Syria. The invasion force sent by Egypt included an armored brigade and an artillery battalion, and Iraq sent a similar sized contingent. In addition to this, Egypt, Iraq and Syria activated their air forces and Egypt also used its navy in the war against the new state.

---

100 Al-Qawukji, a native of Aleppo, Syria, led the "Committee for the Defense of Palestine" in 1936. He organized military training among Arab nationalists, imposing a unified command over the rebel forces. He was an admirer of Adolph Hitler and developed contacts with the Nazi government. After participating in the Vichy defense of Syria he escaped to Germany, where he lived until the end of the war. He eventually made his way back to Syria and become the field commander of the "Arab Liberation Army" of General Sir Ismail Safwar Pasha. Sachar, pp. 200, 209, 299.

My friends and I used to go out at night to protect Rosh ha-Ayin, Beit Badakkah, Kfar Avraham (an eastern neighborhood of Petach Tikva), and other nearby locations, and patrolling along the border.

At the same time, spring, 1948, about a week before the declaration of the state, I separated from my brother-in-law, Yisrael Kaplan, in whose spring factory I had been working, and I opened my own spring factory which I called "Techno-Kefitz" (techno-spring).

One Shabbat, during the synagogue services, Yosef Harel, whom I recognized as a Haganah man, suddenly appeared and said, "We need you. A ship has entered the Haifa harbor carrying machine guns and hand guns from Czechoslovakia and mortars, but their springs are damaged and we urgently need these weapons." My home base in Petach Tikva received an order to release me from guard duty and the commander grumbled, "I finally get an excellent scout and now they take him!" I left the synagogue, got into the car that had come to pick me up and went to recruit five additional workers. Beginning that Shabbat we worked non-stop for three days and two nights. The refurbished mortars went directly from my factory to the fighters in the Negev and Jerusalem. When we finished the work on the mortars we fashioned springs for assembling Miles style grenades. That same night, as soon as the grenades were ready, they were taken to the fighters. At that time, during the peak pressure period, we also worked on Shabbat. This was a clear situation of *pikuach nefesh* (breaking Shabbat laws in order to save lives) and we didn't hesitate in the slightest. The nation in Israel was in danger and I knew that our ability to defend ourselves depended on the immediate supplies of our springs for the fighters' weapons.

Petach Tikva Days

Avraham

I don't have much to tell about our years in Petaḥ Tikva. My memories of that era are based upon a few isolated incidents. So, for example, one year during Rosh Hashanah services the head gabbai, Ben Zion Galis, came over to me and told me quietly, "Rachel Hershler, the wife of Yosef Shmuel Hershler (a *kashrut* supervisor, one of the founders of Petach Tikva), died in Beilinson Hospital. Her funeral will be held in the Segulah Cemetery outside of the city. My elderly worshippers will be unable to undertake this journey. Avraham, you will be the flag bearer (this was the term used in Jerusalem for the rabbi or the head of the *chevra kadisha* [burial society]). Gather ten young men and bring her for burial.

Me with the young generation, from left to right: Me, and on my lap, Nachami, daughter of my brother, Yehudah. To our left, Yossi, son of my sister, Rachel; David, son of my sister Pesha; Avner, son of my sister' Rachel, Yehudah, son of my sister, Pesha; and Goldie, the daughter of my brother Tanchum. Photo taken circa 1943.

The family circa 1946. In the top row from right to left: my brother, Yehudah, Yehudah, the son of my brother Tanchum; my brother Tanchum; my brother Feival; my brother-in-law Yisrael Kaplan, husband of my sister Rachel; and me (the far left). In the middle row from right to left, Yehudit, the wife of my brother Yehudah; my sister, Esther, and on her lap is my daughter Gitti; Aunt Pesha Gavrilovich, my father's sister; my wife, Malkah, and on her lap Yossi, son of my sister Rachel; my sister Pesha and on her lap is Gitta, daughter of my sister, Esther; Shlomo Altman, husband of my sister Pesha. In the bottom row from right to left: Nechami, daughter of my brother Yehudah; Mina, my cousin, daughter of Pesha Gavrilovich; Avner, the son of my sister Rachel; and Yaakov, son of my brother Tanchum.

I went out to the courtyard of the synagogue, gathered a few young men and said to them, "*Chevra*, we have work to do. Go home and recite *kiddush*, and then come back." It is well known that the Torah commands us "not to leave [the body unburied]" and one must conduct the funeral for the deceased on the same day as the death. The young men agreed to my request and soon returned. We went on our way, along with two women who would prepare the body for burial. We went to Beilinson Hospital and from there we headed out to Segulah, and relatively long distance. It was already evening when we got home.

In those days, in the early 1950's, Segulah Cemetery was not terribly large. Next to the place where we buried Mrs. Hershler, z"l, I saw an anonymous grave. This aroused my curiosity and the next day I asked the *gabbai* who the man was. "Don't ask," he answered, and he told me that when Petach Tikva was established the body of a young Jewish man was found hanging from a tree. There were no signs of identification on him, nor papers, but they saw the *tzitzit* under his clothing and brought him for a Jewish burial. On the tombstone they wrote, "Unknown."

Moshe Shmuel Ra'ev, the son of Yehudah Ra'ev,[101] one of the founders and members of the first town council, told about the fears that accompanied the settlers in the early days of Petach Tikva. The settlement was built upon unbroken soil, and there were wild animals and many snakes in the area, including venomous ones. With my own ears I heard him tell that one day his father went out with Yehoshua Stampfer, another founder of Petach Tikva, while they were riding horses, wearing *abbayas* (Arab cloaks).

---

101 Yehudah Ra'ev was a cousin of Yehoshua Stampfer, my great-great grandfather and one of the founders of Petach Tikva. Ra'ev's father, Elazar, was inspired by Rabbi Zvi Kalisher to move to Israel. Yehudah Ra'ev spent two years training in agriculture and self defense, and was a certified teacher of Hungarian before the family moved to Eretz Yisrael in 1875. While the rest of the family waited in Jaffa for a caravan to go to Jerusalem, Yehudah went ahead and hiked alone to Jerusalem, in spite of the danger of bandits. He pitched the first tent in Petach Tikva, dug the first well and was the first guard. He directed the agricultural work of the settlers, most of whom were unfamiliar with farming, and made it clear to their Arab neighbors that they would defend themselves and their property. When Petach Tikva was abandoned in 1883 the family moved to Jerusalem, but they were the first to return to the colony the following year. Ra'ev served as an agricultural consultant to other early settlements, such as Rishon L'tziyon, Hadera and Nes Tsiyona. Tidhar, p. 119-20.

Suddenly one of the horses stepped on a snake, a viper or an adder. The snake rose and began making sounds with his scales. The horse reared in shock, stood on its back legs and from every side more snakes appeared. Stampfer yelled at Ra'ev, "Throw the *abbaya!*" They threw the *abbayas* on the snakes and managed to get away from there without injury. Two weeks later the two of them returned to that spot and found their *abbayas* completely full of holes. The snakes had bitten them and the poison ate through the cloth. Moshe Shmuel Ra'ev heard these things from his father and believed them. As far as anyone knows, snake venom doesn't disintegrate cloth, so chances are that this story contains just a bit of exaggeration. In any event, it's a story worth telling and adds a flourish to the aura that surrounded the lives of the founders of Petach Tikva.

Our family married into the Stampfer family: My sister, Nechama, married one of the grandsons of Yehoshua Stampfer and my brother, Tanchum, married one of his granddaughters, as I will describe later.

Malka and I in the 1960's.

We wanted to leave Petach Tikva. I had had enough of the long bus trip from home to work in Tel Aviv, and in particular was fed up with waiting in the long line of passengers each morning at the bus station.

In 1957, after the Sinai Campaign, we left Petach Tikva and returned to live in Tel Aviv. We bought an apartment on 1 Itamar ben Avi Street. The two contractors who built the house lived there themselves, and one of them served in the army with my brother Ya'akov, and they remained friends. So we had confidence in them and bought the apartment from them.

On weekdays I used to pray in the synagogue on Hashmonaim Street, on the corner of Yehudah Halevi. This was a small synagogue which shared a common wall with a ruined water reservoir which had earlier served to water the orchards which dotted the area. But on Shabbat and holidays we prayed in the Bilu Synagogue at 124 Rothchild Avenue, which was affiliated with a boy's school where our sons learned.

THE BILU SYNAGOGUE

Welcoming a new Torah scroll at the Bilu synagogue (I am holding the staff on the right hand side.

The founder of the Bilu School for Boys, of the Mizrachi movement, was Rabbi Chayim Meshori, the father of Shimon Meshori, who later became the first violinist in the Israel Radio Orchestra. It's impossible to talk about this synagogue without noting the wonderful and impressive prayers held in conjunction with the synagogue's youth choir. The choir was led by Cantor Shlomo Ravitz, z"l, who was the lead cantor in the great synagogue of Tel Aviv.

After his death at the remarkable age of over 100 years, it was led by the cantors: Yosef Malvani, Menashe Lev Ran and Mordecai Sobel, each of whom in his own way carved a brilliant career in the cantorial world. The congregation used to join in the choir's singing and enjoyed a moving musical experience which left its mark for many years in the memories of all who came to that synagogue.

I served as *gabbai* in this remarkable synagogue for years, and during that time many visitors came to enjoy the prayers and the singing. The visitors included many high ranking individuals: presidents of different countries, diplomats, artists, and leading public figures from Israel and abroad. Among the women, I remember the actress Channa Rovina, Knesset member and winner of the 1968 Israel prize, Shoshana Parsitz, Sima Arlosoroff, widow of the statesman Chaim Arlosoroff, and others.[102]

WE CELEBRATED BAR MITZVAHS BY CALLING THE YOUNG men up to the Torah, and their parents—even non-religious families—would ask us months in advance if they could hold their event in our synagogue. Rabbis gave sermons on the holidays and I especially recall Rabbi Shmuel Zanwill Kahana, z"l, the director general of the Ministry of Religion, whose absorbing and inspiring sermons I will never forget. On the High Holydays, particularly the night of *Kol Nidre*,

---

[102] The murder of labor leader Ḥaim Arlosoroff on a Tel Aviv beach, June 16, 1933 remains a source of dispute in Israel. Three Etzel members were arrested and charged with the murder, but they were later aquitted for lack of evidence. Despite this aquittal suspicions remained that Etzel engineered this murder in retaliation for negotiations between Arlosoroff and the Nazi government in an attempt to bring German Jews to Israel. In 1983 then Prime Minister Begin reopened the case. A special commission sifted through the evidence and in 1985 concluded that the Revisionist Etzel was not to blame, nor was the labor party guilty of blood libel in return. http://archive.jta.org/article/1985/06/17/3001714/52-years-after-arlosoroff-murder-panel-clears-3-revisionist-suspects

the synagogue was completely filled and even Rothchild Boulevard teemed with people who couldn't find a place to sit inside. They'd gather in groups outside to hear the prayer and the exquisite songs of the youth choir.

My position as *gabbai* gave me the chance to meet interesting people from Israel and abroad. I remember one Shabbat a stranger appeared in the synagogue, a camera hanging on his arm. I went over to him to tell him that photography wasn't allowed on Shabbat, and he told me that he was a tourist from Sweden who had come to Israel with a group of teachers who went to Eilat for the weekend. He, however, was interested in the experience of Jewish life and they suggested that he come to the Bilu Synagogue. After the services, I invited him to come to our house for a Shabbat meal, and he happily accepted. His joy was doubled and tripled when he tasted the delicious food from Malkah's kitchen, and was told that all of the food was strictly kosher and had been prepared on Friday before Shabbat began. He especially enjoyed the *cholent* and the sweet melodies of the family's *zemirot* (Shabbat songs).[103] When he returned to Sweden he sent us an enthusiastic letter, and stressed that he would never forget the experience of that Shabbat and that that Shabbat was the crown jewel of his visit to the Holy Land.

---

103 Outstanding food prepared by Dodah Malka and outstanding zemirot (Shabbat songs) from Dod Avram are my dominant memories of Shabbat visits to their home in Tel Aviv. Dod Avram knew more melodies than anyone else I ever met, and his booming resonant voice was irresistible.

Chapter Six

The Techno-Kefitz Plant and "A Lively Inanimate Object"

(davar met sheyesh bo ruach chayim)

The Techno-Kefitz plant, which I established during the War of Independence at Derech Petach Tikva 27, supplied springs to the defense forces for 30

years: at first to the Haganah and Etzel, and afterwards to Tzahal (mostly for the Uzi machine gun and the air force), to Rafael[104] and the military industry. I solved innumerable technical and mechanical problems that cropped up for them. My brother Yaakov was my partner at the beginning, and my nephew Amiram, my sister Rachel's son, eventually bought the enterprise when I retired. Whenever I've been asked to define my profession and describe the essence of the spring, I'd say: "It's a lively inanimate object." [דבר מת שיש בו רוח חיים]

In 1982, when I retired, Techno-Kefitz moved to the Barkan industrial area near the city of Ariel in the Shomron region. And when my nephew decided to sell the place, I supported his move wholeheartedly, without any hesitation or regret. Now that I am no longer working I am never bored. I have time to read, I don't have to worry about getting raw materials, repairing machines or devices, orders, improving technical efficiency, taking care of time sheets, paying workers, paying invoices from suppliers, and so on and so forth. It's very difficult to run a manufacturing business, especially in Israel.

At its height I employed 40 workers at Techno-Kefitz. During school vacation times I also employed 15 young men, at the request of my good friend, a fellow congregant at the Bilu synagogue and regional judge, so as to teach these teenagers a trade and keep them out of trouble.

I personally looked after each worker in the plant. I never delayed salaries at Techno-Kefitz and never turned down any worker who wished to meet personally with me. We celebrated happy occasions together and pulled

---

104 Arms Development Authority, which is government owned. http://www.jewishvirtuallibrary.org/jsource/Economy/eco1.html

through sad times as one. Over the years they were all able to buy apartments and establish themselves. One of the workers had triplets. He arrived at work overwhelmed and anxious. "Don't worry," I said to him and I bought him supplies for three babies and three cribs. He never forgot the help I extended to him and reminds me of it every time we happen to meet.

I always believed in the verse, "Cast your bread upon the waters, for in later days you will find it." (Ecclesiasties11:1) I always operated according to this principle and, indeed, in later days there were results I never could have imagined. So, for example, when I worked for Etzel and Lechi I refused to accept payments. First of all, because they had no money and secondly, because their problems were usually quite simple to solve: repairing a spring on a mine or some kind of weapon. The Haganah, on the other hand, had needs on a much larger scale, and a corresponding budget. I saw the reward for my labor when they placed increased orders for spring production.

ENGINEERS AND WEAPONS MANUFACTURERS CAME TO my factory. David Leibowitz, the Haganah man who developed the "Davidka" mortar, planned its springs with me. Before he left the plant with the springs he said to me, "You will hear the shots very well." And indeed the psychological impact of the noise of the Davidka was much greater than its power of destruction, and the Arabs thought it was a secret and deadly force. The Davidka was first used in March, 1948 during an attack on the Abu Kabir neighborhood in Jaffa. My brother Yaakov then served as a commander at the air field in Lod for the Haganah and heard the shots. He saw Iraqi and Syrian soldiers approaching Jaffa and thought that they were the attackers. He got in touch with me and asked, "Who is shelling whom?" I said, "Don't worry, it's us shelling them."

SOMEONE ELSE WHO CAME TO MY FACTORY WAS ALEK Sokochover, a Palmach man and father of Amos Chorev, the chief of reserves. Sokochover was an engineer who had an outstanding ability for technical improvisation. During the first cease fire they brought him to me especially from Jerusalem.[105] He designed a navy torpedo, whose first mission was to attack a British destroyer and prevent the deportation of refugees from the ship *The Exodus* to Europe in July, 1947.[106] Everything was prepared. Many officers were stationed along the beach, including Yigal Allon, but at the last minute a telegram came from Ben

---

105 David Ben Gurion announced Israel's declaration of independence on Friday afternoon, Mary 14, 1948—the day the British officially withdrew from the land. War broke out immediately. A four-week truce, brokered by the United Nations, began on June 11, 1948. On July 10, 1948, the war was renewed and lasted ten days. The second truce began on July 19, 1948 and held until October 15th of that year. The third cease-fire came into effect on October 22. An armistice was finally signed between Israel and Egypt on February 24, 1949, with Lebanon on March 23, and with Transjordan on April 3, 1949. All were arranged under the auspices of the United Nations mediator Dr. Ralph Bunche, and the United Nations. Gilbert, pp. 186, 208-9, 216, 233, 248

106 This is not to be confused with the subject of Leon Uris' book, *Exodus*. In July, 1947, a ferry boat loaded with 4500 Holocaust survivors, tried to run the British blockade as part of the "illegal immigration" run by the Haganah. The ship was intercepted by the British, a struggle ensued and three Jews were killed. The crew surrendered when the British began ramming the boat, threatening to sink it. The ferry was towed into Haifa and the British decided to return the refugees to their port of embarkation, instead of taking them to internment camps in Cyprus, where 26,000 DPs (displaced persons) were already straining the camps' capacities. The Jewish passengers decided not to accept their banishment with docility and British soldiers used rifle butts, hose pipes and tear gas against the survivors during their forcible transfer to another ship and they were eventually sent back to Hamburg, Germany. This tragedy, which extended over three months, was widely covered in newspapers throughout the world and profoundly influenced world opinion towards supporting the establishment of a Jewish state. Gilbert, pp.145-46; Sachar, pp.282-283.

Gurion canceling the mission out of fears of diplomatic fallout from such an action.

On April 25, 1948, an Etzel battalion began an attack on northern Jaffa, with the goal of capturing the heavily fortified Manshia neighborhood.[107] The attack was accompanied by a heavy bombardment which provoked a large portion of the Arab population to flee the city. During the course of the battle some problems developed with their weapons and the Etzel men brought them to my factory for repair. We succeeded in resolving the problem within an hour and the fighters returned to Jaffa. On April 28 Etzel renewed the attack and managed to cut off the Manshia neighborhood from the city. That night the Haganah began "Operation Chametz," to encircle the city. By May 1, the city was surrounded. In the coming days almost all of the Arab population abandoned the city. (Only 4,000 of the 100,000 Arab residents remained in the city). On May 13th the city leaders signed a surrender agreement.

Malkah

Avraham got his first reserve draft order in the 1950's. A soldier came to our house and gave the order to our daughter Gitti. I knew that I had to quickly notify Avraham; back then there was a telephone at the factory, but there were no residential phones. I went to the pharmacy, which had a phone, and I called the plant. Yaakov, Avraham's brother, answered and I asked, "Please let me speak with Avraham."

Avraham came to the phone and asked, "Who is this?"

---

107 This operation began with an Irgun assault, but after two days they requested that this become a joint Irgun/Haganah operation. Arab Jaffa surrendered in May 13, 1948, just one day before the proclamation of Israel's independence, and immediately upon the withdrawal of the last British troops from Jaffa. Gilbert, pp.175-76, 183.

"Somebody you meet with every day," I answered.

"There's no one like that!" he answered with confidence. This was the first time we had ever spoken on the telephone and he didn't recognize my voice. "Actually, there is!" I said, laughing. From then on it was enough for one of us to whisper, "There's no one like that," and we'd break out laughing with the memory.

Avraham

Shortly after the War of Independence, maybe in 1949, I found out that my friend from the Haganah unit in the Old City, Nahum Gershonowitz, was being sent by the Jewish Agency to Tunisia. I entrusted him with some money and asked him to send me springs from tanks and artillery that remained abandoned in Tunisia after World War II. Gershonowitz managed to gather a sizeable amount of springs, packed them up in 12 metal packing cases and shipped them to the Port of Haifa. He wrote to me giving the details of the shipment and when the time came I happily went to pick up my merchandise from the Port of Haifa.

The clerk in the port, who could scarcely be bothered to lift his head from the table, asked, "Do you have a permit?"

"What do I need a permit for?" I was astonished. "Now we have our own state. I understand paying duty, but permission? Why?" It became clear that I was naïve and wasn't aware of the new bureaucratic arrangements.

I had no alternative but to turn to the engineer Chaim Salvin, the director of Israel Defense Industries. Already in 1946 Ben Gurion had instructed Salvin to bring in weapon machinery disguised as scrap iron from the United States to Israel. Bringing these supplies to Israel despite the scrutiny of the Mandate inspectors permitted the establishment of weapon and ammunition industries during the sanctions that existed during the War of Independence. On a number of occasions Salvin asked me to create a spring for some new weapon or help him develop different devices, so we had close and friendly relations.

Chaim Salvin vouched for me and the packing cases arrived two weeks later. I sorted the springs and Tzahal officers started visiting the plant when they needed the right type of spring for artillery or vehicles that they had captured, so they could be made operational.

Some time later I received a letter from Chaim Salvin which testifies to the close and flexible rapport which characterized our relationship.

Among the rest, Salvin wrote: "I know that the price should be much higher, but I'm glad that you give me the opportunity to pay even something ... it is not so good that I pay less than I should, but it is very pleasant that young men of your caliber still exist. Sometimes I think you are the last of the Mohicans."

In 1953, five years after the establishment of the State, Heyman Shamir and Al Schwimmer paid a quick visit to my factory. Shamir was a pilot, whom I knew from the Haganah. He introduced me to Al Schwimmer, a well established American Jew who transferred his residence to Israel in order to help build the fledgling state.[108] They told me that they were

---

[108] "In 1948 Schwimmer and his friend Hank Greenspun (later a Las Vegas newspaper publisher) stole into a military surplus base stacked with weapons and ammunition from World War II—and through a daring series of events, arranged for this stolen material to reach Israel ... Schwimmer was tried by the Justice Department for violating the Neutrality Act, which prohibited weapons being sent to Israel. He was found guilty, but the judge refused to sentence him to jail. He was finally pardoned by President Bill Clinton in 2000, 52 years later... In 1950 Schwimmer was managing a small airport outside Los Angeles when a car drew up and out stepped David Ben Gurion, the first Prime Minister of Israel. Ben Gurion convinced Schwimmer to come to Israel and start Israel Aircraft Industries ...He died in Israel at the age of 95. http://www.forbes.com/sites/robertlenzner/2011/06/12/al-schwimmer-an-american-crucial-to-the-state-of-israel/.

on their way to the government offices to recommend that Ben Gurion build a factory to repair and improve aircraft. Two hours later they stopped on their way back and told me that Ben Gurion agreed, and that they had received a green light. So the two of them became the founders of the Israel Aircraft Industry. At first they called the operation "Badak," later changing it to "Aircraft Industries." We maintained professional connections throughout the coming years. (Heyman Shamir was sent to Czechoslovakia in August, 1948, during the War of Independence, to examine Spitfire airplanes which the air force had purchased. He and a friend examined the planes and the spare parts, conducted repairs and preparations and then organized "Operation Velvet" to fly the planes to Israel. I heard that on the way back they flew over Egypt, encountered some Egyptian planes and downed them.)

Around that time the military industry began to develop an Israeli gun called the "Dror" in cooperation with the American firm, Johnson. An expert engineer came from America in order to supervise the development and manufacturing. He came to my factory to see where and how the springs were manufactured. He was impressed and advised the Military Industry people: "You have someone you can depend on. The tools and machinery that Frank has are at American standards." However, he pointed out that Israel had too many planners and too few producers. At the end of his visit he said: "You are like a family who is concerned about a sick member; everyone prescribes a different treatment and in the meantime the sick person dies."

Before the Six Day War I worked night and day for the ordnance corps, the air force Israel Defense Industries and Rafael (the Arms Development Authority). During the waiting period [the two weeks or so before the war actually began] when nerves were stretched thin, when the State was threatened on three sides by three large armies (by Jordan, Egypt and Syria), I was invited to visit a few bases to get a close up impression of the war preparations.[109] During the course of one long day I visited Tzahal camps. I saw the condition of the weaponry, the ammunition and the administration of the units—and I was very impressed. When I came home I told everybody that if the war broke out we would win, and the war would last only five days. People made fun of me and claimed that I was fantasizing and suffered from wishful thinking. But when the war ended in a crushing victory those scoffers complained: "Avraham, you made a mistake. You said five days and the war ended up lasting six days!"

ON SHABBAT, BEFORE THE WAR BROKE OUT, WE MET WITH the cantor David Bagli who came from America to visit my brother-in-law Rabbi Gronum Lando, husband of my sister Minah. The cantor was concerned because all the flights to and from Israel had been cancelled and he was unable to leave. "Don't worry," I said to him, "in another week you'll be able to return to America and even before then you'll be able to visit the Western Wall." A year later the cantor returned to visit Israel, and this time he sought me out and wanted to thank me. "I salute you," he said. "When everyone was trembling in fear and tension, you believed that we'd succeed, and you put hope and confidence in my heart."

---

109 I well remember those weeks during our sabbatical year in Israel. Most of our teachers, as well as bus drivers and other familiar figures, were called up for army reserve duty. We prepared our apartment by taping and painting the windows, clearing out and stocking our shelter and practiced war drills in school.

Once some ordnance officers came to my factory and presented me with a problem they had interchanging [gun] magazines. "Avraham," they requested, "solve this problem for us." They brought two magazines from Kalachnikov rifles connected one to the other in an improvised manner, with a strip of cloth and wire. The challenge was to bind them so that when one magazine was emptied, it would be easy to quickly remove it and insert the second one. I invented a "magazine connector"—a steel spring that held both magazines together. The minute one magazine was emptied, you'd take it out, replace it with the second one that's attached to it, and within a few seconds you can start shooting again.

A few years later someone came into the factory bringing a familiar looking spring with him and wanted to order 10,000 more. I immediately recognized my work and identified it as a "magazine connector." I realized that he was bidding for the ministry of defense contract, and some reason they didn't include me, and the tender was held without my knowledge. I got in touch with the Ordnance commander. "Who wants him?" asked the secretary. "Major Frank," I answered. He came to the phone immediately and asked, "Avraham, how are things going?" I told him that someone was going around with a sample of my invention and I reminded him of the words of the prophet: "I remember the kindness of your youth," (Jeremiah 2:2)." I had invented and built the magazine connector at no charge and now a tender was offered by the Ministry of Defense and I was not included. He was upset. The next day a messenger with papers arrived, and asked me to sign to my willingness to participate in the tender. I was so angry that I didn't want to sign, but the messenger refused to leave, saying: "They told me not to come back to the Ministry of Defense without your signature." In the end I agreed to participate in the bidding.

ONE DAY A YOUNG MAN NAMED UZI GAL CAME TO Techno-Kefitz. He told me about an idea he had to design a compact submachine gun and wanted me to create the springs for him. I worked on all of the prototype springs for him at no charge until we hit upon the most functional and efficient design. Eventually, in 1955, when the development of the Uzi submachine gun was completed, it became a hit both in Israel and abroad and the military industry started producing them in large quantities, the specifications stated explicitly that the springs needed to be ordered from Techno-Kefitz.

THE ISRAELI INSTITUTE OF STANDARDS TURNED TO ME, as they did to other companies, with a request to supervise the manufacturing procedures. I'd have to pay membership dues of 6,000 lire a year, a significant sum at the time, so that they could inspect and certify the products I was developing. I refused to pay, and didn't agree to the presence of their people in the research area, since we were talking about industrial secrets that took a long time to fully develop. However, I gladly agreed that they inspect the final products. My answer was not agreeable to the Institute of Standards and they turned to the military industries, demanding that they no longer work with Techno-Kefitz since it refused to pay membership dues and wouldn't allow them to be present during the manufacturing process. The military industries people, who had known me since the days of the underground, and knew the value of the products I manufactured, turned a deaf ear to this order, saying: "We will continue to work with Frank even without the Institute of Standards."

Professor Boaz Popper, one of the founders of Rafael, and a highly regarded inventor, once told me, concerning a certain spring, "Avraham, if you hadn't succeeded in making the spring, we would have been unable to develop the product." I think that the patent is still pending for this product, so I'll only say that it has to do with bomb manufacture.

One day an Arab came to my plant, and in his hand he held a spring. "I need you to make a spring like this for me, and it must be made exactly like the sample." "What is it for?" I asked, even though I identified it immediately as a spring for a German Mauser pistol. "It's for a sewing machine," he answered and asked me to set a day and time when he could come and pick up the merchandise.

I prepared three springs for him that were amazingly precise, but he would never use them: I added a secret spring which would prevent the pistol's [accurate] aim. I had let the Defense Services know that we were talking about a punctual Arab, and that he would come on certain day and time to get the springs. The Arab arrived at the set hour, took the springs, paid for them and I raised my cap so that those who were following him would know that this was the target. The people of the Defense Services trailed him and found in his home an extraordinary stockroom full of weapons, including an impressive array of guns and pistols.

Chapter Seven

May the Memory of the Righteous be a Blessing

Abba passed from this world on the 21st of Kislev, 1961. One of the leading rabbis wrote about him: "In the holiness and splendor of his Torah, our rabbi was like the Holy Ark, which contained within it the Tablets of Testimony, written on both sides, the Written Law and the Oral Law, and its departure has created a spiritual void."

My father on his final journey, winter 1960.

After his death, and at the initiative of Dr. Yitzchak Nevenzal, who was the second comptroller of the State, the Rav Frank Institute was established in Jerusalem. It was headed by Rabbi Yitzchak Rosenthal, who was Abba's secretary for many decades. After his death, his son, Rabbi Shabbetai Rosenthal, took his place. The institute set a goal of collecting Abba's life work and publishing them. Drawing upon his judicial rulings, ledgers, letters and notebooks, and thousands of notes which Abba left behind, seven publications of responsa and halakhic research have been published, eight publications about the Jewish holidays, seven volumes of his responsa *Har Zvi*, and many other publications of legal decisions.

After Abba's death Rabbi Shabbetai Rosenthal wrote about him: "His written Torah was found in his responsa, *Har Zvi*, *Mikraei Kodesh*, (about the holidays) and more. Rabbi Zvi Pesach was among those who paved the road for the emerging decisions regarding the *mitzvot* that apply in Israel, and was the head of the *Midrash B'nei Tziyon*, where the great rabbis of Jerusalem dealt with determining these laws, and publishing the volumes of *Kerem Tziyon*. He also dealt deeply with the laws regarding the Temple, and in the wake of the religious enthusiasm that took root after Israel was taken over by the British, Rav Zvi Pesach wrote the book, *Mikdash Melech*, on the subject of renewing the sacrificial system. Rav Zvi Pesach was quite involved in leading the public during the period when divisive disputes began in the Holy Land. He had great fondness for observant farmers, like the settlers of Gush Etzion, some of whom had studied in his *beit midrash*. He supported the growth of Jewish defense from its very outset, and in the final days of the Mandate, his house contained hiding places for weapons and underground activities.[110] Rav Zvi Pesach joined with Rav Kook in establishing the rabbinate and rabbinical courts, and resisting the spread of secular influences. He saw the hand of God in the nation's development in the land, but continuously fought for Torah observance in the State: such as opposing the conscription of women and yeshiva students, the laws of "Who is a Jew" and so forth. Rav Zvi Pesach saw the hour of Israel's independence as an amazing opportunity from heaven, but at the same time he continuously sought that 'the law of the Torah be the law of the State of Israel, for all practical purposes.'"

ABBA CAME OUT WITH CREATIVE RELIGIOUS RULINGS which supported everyday Zionism. He took an activist's path in finding ingenious halachic solutions that would permit a religious Jew to keep the laws of the land and the laws of *halacha* without damaging his income. So, for example, in B'nei Brak, when fruits and vegetables were imported from outside Israel during the *shemittah* year (the sabbatical year when Jews were forbidden to work the land) Abba suggested leasing the land to non-Jews and to work them again at the end of the year. And this is but one example among many.

In the 1950's a conflict broke out between Chassidic and Mitnagid Jews regarding the sale of holy objects, which requires a special halakhic dispensation. The two sides

---

110 One of our family's favorite stories took place while my parents were living with Rav Frank in 1947. British soldiers came into the house to search for weapons. Mom was outraged that they'd invade the home of such a respected rabbi. When the soldiers came across the trunk my parents had brought from America, they started tearing it apart, strewing garments and other items about the room. They found no weapons, and Mom yelled at them, "Look at this mess! You'd better clean it up!" Mom is barely 4"11—small and mighty—and they listened to her. "Sorry, mum," one mumbled, handing her his gun. And he cleaned it up.

turned to Abba for a *din Torah* (legal ruling according to halacha), and he decided what he decided. But the Chassidim were not satisfied and the disputants turned to the *Chazon Ish*.[111] The *Chazon Ish*, Rabbi Avraham Yishaya Korelitz of B'nai Brak, and my father had a friendly relationship, full of mutual respect and esteem. The *Chazon Ish* ruled what he ruled, and one of the mitnagdim said, "That's exactly what Rav Frank ruled." When the *Chazon Ish* heard this he berated them, saying, "You dare to come to me after Rav Frank already gave you his ruling? Have you no shame?" In that way he passed along an unambiguous message of honor and respect for Abba and the importance of accepting his decisions without appeal.

AFTER MY FATHER'S DEATH I RECITED *KADDISH* FOR HIM in the synagogue on Chashmonaim Street in Tel Aviv. One of the neighbors, Reb Yaakov Menzaleh, a learned man originally from Aden in Yemen, came over to see who was reading in such a loud voice. When he heard that I was a son of Rabbi Frank he was quite moved and told me that in 1925 he had served as the *Safra D'dina* (secretary of the Beit Din) in Calcutta. At that time the Indian courts dealt with a long and complicated case which began when a wealthy Jew passed away, leaving behind a large inheritance worth millions of pound sterling and much property. The heirs quarreled, and sought legal intervention in order to arbi-

---

111 Rav Yeshaya Korelitz, 1858-1953 was a major leader of the haredi community in Israel. He came to Eretz Yisrael in 1933, moving to Bnai Brak. He placed a great emphasis on Torah learning and strict observance of *mitzvot*. Although he opposed Zionism, he avoided political entanglements, concentrating instead on promoting Jewish education and yeshivot. Like many rabbis, he is known by the title of a book he authored, a commentary on the *Shulchan Aruch* called *Hazon Ish*. http://www.yivoencyclopedia.org/article.aspx/Karelits_Avraham_Yeshayahu

trate between the disputants. The legal wrangling lasted ten years, moving from one court to another, and none of the judges were able to rule in the matter. Finally, in 1935, the case reached the supreme court of India and they concluded that the case should be decided according to Jewish law and so they needed to consult with an expert in that field. They turned to Abba, and he agreed to advise them regarding the complex situation. He took a train from Jerusalem to Alexandria and from there, a ship through the Suez Canal to India. He was accompanied by Mordechai Eliash, a religious Jew who was one of the outstanding attorneys in Israel in those days, and also by my sister Pesha, who came along to help Abba during his one month journey.

After learning the details and the complications which had arisen, Abba suggested a *halachic* solution to resolve the dispute. The supreme court of India (which functioned, as in Israel, according British law), accepted the decision and so, at long last, an appropriate way was found to divide the inheritance.

Abba's decision became a precedent and won great praise in the Indian judicial world, in Israel and in England. Rav Yaakov Menzaleh told me, "I am deeply moved to answer *amen* for the Kaddish in memory of your father, of blessed memory, a holy man."

WE WERE ONCE INVITED TO A FESTIVE EVENT HELD AT the music department at the Hebrew University, in honor of a significant gift by Morris Wosk, a Canadian donor. I knew Morris Wosk through the son of my sister Channah, Abie Sacks, who lived in Vancouver [British Columbia]. When Wosk came for a visit in Israel, my nephew asked me to help him find a place in a synagogue for Rosh Hashanah. Thus began a long lasting friendship between us. Since then we have hosted Wosk and his family in our home every time they visited Israel, and when his son celebrated his *bar mitzvah*, he was called to the Torah in the Bilu Synagogue. Among the invitees was also a supreme court judge, Moshe Landuo, an amateur pianist who played in a quartet together with the donor's wife. The donor introduced us and said to the judge: "Please meet Mr. Frank." "Do you have any connection with Rabbi Frank?" he asked, and I answered, "I am his son." Judge Landuo stood up. "The honor is mine, I stand when I mention his name. Your father was a great man."

Years after his death I would still meet people who knew and honored Abba. One day there was a newspaper announcement from Egged (the bus company) which included a letter to the company from Abba at the height of the unrest (in 1936). In his rich and descriptive language Abba thanked the company, praising their actions and stressing the courage of its drivers.

ABBA DIRECTED US TO MAINTAIN A SET TIME OF STUDY when we would learn holy texts and words of Torah, each of us according to his time and ability. So too he always urged us to treat others with patience and gentleness, to work towards the observance of our heritage and the unity of the nation. Abba acted according to these principles all the days of his life.

I, who had the honor of being the son of one of the great rabbis of his generation, have remained faithful to his spirit and legacy. He bequeathed his love of books, and so I have decided to include a poem for Rosh Hashanah, written by

Zechariah, who is Yechiya, son of Saadiah Altzahari, one of the great poets of Yemen. In 1567 Zacharia visited Israel and wrote a composition of rich language and wonderful rhyme which draws upon juxtaposition of words not just from scripture, but from Talmudic literature.

[I'm not even going to attempt translating this poem!!]

Chapter Eight

My Brothers and Sisters

MY OLDEST SISTER, CHANNAH

In 1912 there was talk about arranging a match for my oldest sister, Channah. My father arranged a match between her and Menachem Bentzion Sacks, a young scholar, the great-great-grandson of Reb Moshe Sacks. Reb Moshe Sacks came to Israel from Germany in 1820, and was one of the forces behind the building of the Battei Machse neighborhood. He established an Ashkenazi *minyan* in the Old City, meeting in a private home praying according to the Ashkenazic manner. Up until that time all of the synagogues in Jerusalem prayed with the Sephardic liturgy, according to the Chassidic tradition. Reb Moshe Sacks was the father of Yitzchak, who, in turn, was the father of Avraham Elkanah Sacks. Elkanah's son was Dov Ber Sacks, who was the father of Menachem Bentzion Sacks who married my sister, Channah.

*Ida, the dear daughter of my sister Channah,
with my daughter Gitti (on the right)*

After the birth of their third child, and in the face of the difficult economic circumstances in Jerusalem during the First World War, Menachem Bentzion Sacks went to America with only the shirt on his back, to find a living as a rabbi or teacher. As expected, he met with difficulties at the outset, but within a few months he was employed as a rabbi in a Chicago yeshiva. In the meantime, my sister and her children stayed behind in Jerusalem, pining for him until my mother said to her: "Even though it pains me to separate from you, your husband is in America—you must go to America. Without a husband there is no life."

In Chicago, Menachem Bentzion became recognized as an accomplished speaker. He was also blessed with organizational ability that helped move his community forward and allowed the expansion of its institutions. He built study houses (*battei midrash*), *yeshivas* and *talmud torahs* (elementary schools). Rabbis from around the world came to stay with him and learned, among other lessons, a thing or two about raising funds for their own *yeshivas*. Once a year he would receive a visit from Rabbi Yosef Shlomo Kahaneman, the founder of the Ponovitz Yeshiva in Bnai Brak, and the Gaon Rabbi Meir Shapiro from Lublin, one of the leading rabbis of Poland, the head of Yeshiva Chochmei Lublin and the founder of *Daf Yomi* (a plan to study a page of *talmud* a day). The house of Menachem Bentzion and my sister Channah became a meeting place for scholars, open and welcoming to all.[112]

My sister Channah died during one of her visits to Israel and was buried on Har Menuchot. Her husband named the first Jewish school he established in Chicago after her, and it still exists, "Channah Sacks." Likewise, he also established a fund that gives prizes to outstanding educators. Menachem Bentzion Sacks lived in America for about 50 years, and when he passed away, he was brought to Jerusalem for burial.

My Sisters Sarah and Rivkaleh and My Brother Zalman

My sister Sarah was born in 1898 and died the year I was born, in 1917, at the height of the First World War. She was only 17 years old when she died. My sister Rivkaleh and my brother Zalman also died at an early age. For many years Imma used to go up to the Mount of Olives to visit the graves of her three children who were taken from her before their time.

---

112 The Chicago Jewish News named Rabbi Sacks among Chicago's top 100 Jews of the twentieth century. www.chicagojewishnews.com/lists_chijews.htm

My Brother Tanchum

My brother Tanchum, the oldest of the boys, was born in 1899. At the time he was born the population of Jerusalem was about 40,000 souls. Two-thirds of the inhabitants of Jerusalem were Jews, and the rest were Muslim or Christian. The land itself was governed by the Ottoman Empire.

When he was a boy, about eight or nine years old, Tanchum went out to the courtyard and saw a necktie lying on the ground. He bent down to pick it up and it moved. It was none other than a small poisonous snake which quickly slithered into the house. The parents didn't know what to do and turned to someone from their synagogue who knew how to trap snakes. He came to the house and worked his magic. Like a snake charmer who lulls a snake with his whispers so it will not strike, as it is written, "Their venom is like that of a snake, a deaf viper that stops its ears, so as not to hear the voice of charmers or the expert mutterer of spells." (Psalms 58:5-6). Having completed his work, he went on his way, holding the snake in his hands.

Imma told me another story of a snake which caused many troubles during the days of hunger and deprivation in Jerusalem during the First World War. At that time eggs were a scarce commodity and only a few had the luxury of buying them. A Jewish merchant of Jerusalem used to buy eggs and store them in a metal container in his house. To his astonishment he discovered that from time to time the eggs would disappear. He turned to Rabbi Shmuel Salant, the rabbi of Jerusalem, and the rabbi suggested that he hard boil a few eggs and then put them on top of the other eggs. The merchant followed his advice and a few days later he found a cobra which had choked on a hardboiled egg. A fitting end to the thief.

Tanchum married Shoshana, a granddaughter of Reb Yehoshua Stampfer, one of the founders of Petaḥ Tikva. For 42 years Tanchum worked devotedly and conscientiously for the chief rabbinate, which primarily dealt with matters of personal status. His reputation preceded him as a morally scrupulous man, upright and faithful, an enlightened and knowledgeable scholar, and he was without pretentions towards honor and high office. He dealt gently with everyone, honestly and fairly, despising laziness and negligence, and for this reason he was honored and esteemed by everyone who knew him.

In 1941, when Abba underwent an operation in Tel Aviv, and the house was left empty most of the day, two young men appeared in the Rabbinate offices. They wanted to speak with Tanchum. "Please," my brother said to them, "What is the problem?"

"No, we want to speak with you privately," they mumbled.

Tanchum took them to a side office and the two told him that they had broken into the house and stole silver utensils and other items. Only now did they realize that this was the house of Rabbi Frank, and since then they were seized with fear and their spirits found no rest. All they wanted was to return the stolen objects. Tanchum explained to them the significance of true and honest repentance, he spoke to them as an educator and teacher, without shaming or humiliating them, and he did not turn them over to the police. He allowed them to return the items, which turned out to be utensils the family used for Passover.[113]

---

113 Dod Tanḥum was a very dignified and gentle personage. My brother Shaul made a point of visiting him every motzei Shabbat for many years. I went with him a few times, and shared the impression of a gracious and modest man. As Shaul says, it's very challenging to be the son of a great man, and Tanḥum was able to do that with great integrity and dignity.

My Sister Nechama

Nechama married Eliyahu David Stampfer, the older brother of Shoshana, Tanchum's wife. In the face of the difficult economic circumstances Eliyahu David decided to follow in the footsteps of his brother-in-law, Menachem Bentzion Sacks, and go to America to seek employment. He went from one place to another in the United States, finally becoming the chief rabbi of Akron, Ohio.[114] Nechama and her two sons, Joshua and Judah, joined him and my sister was energetically involved in community activities within the community and in the Hadassah organization. Their grandson, Shaul Stampfer, moved to Israel and serves a professor of history in the Hebrew University of Jerusalem.[115]

Tragically, Nechama was killed in an automobile accident in the summer of 1939. Forty-one years later, in 1980, her body was brought for burial on the Mount of Olives.

---

114 My grandparents indeed had a difficult time. For a few years my grandfather served as rabbi at the Baron Hirsch Synagogue in Memphis, Tennessee. In Akron he was the "rav kehilla," the community rabbi, serving several small congregations on a rotating basis. One of my dad's childhood nightmare memories was the week following his bar mitzvah. The people of the shul next on rotation were wishing a mazel tov on the bar mitzvah and my grandfather, proud of his son, volunteered him to read the *hafatara*—without any preparation on my father's part. Ever since then my dad has always looked over the *haftara* when he'd get to *shul*—just in case!

115 With the last name of "Stampfer," Shaul can't escape the connection that people make with the Stampfer family of Petach Tikva. But many friends remained unaware that Rav Frank was our great-grandfather. I remember visiting one of Shaul's professors back in the day and in the course of conversation Rav Frank's name came up. Just as I was about to open my mouth I got a little kick on my ankle. Shaul didn't want his *yichus* (lineage) intruding.

With my sister Nechama during her visit to Israel, at a vacation village in Motza, 1936.

During the War of Independence, Joshua and Judah, the two sons of Nechama and Eliyahu Stampfer came to Israel to be part of the fighting force.[116] Joshua was assigned to the platoon of the Palmach who set out on January 15, 1948 to aid Gush Etzion.[117] The Gush had been under siege for several months already, and the supply convoys sent to them from Jerusalem had not been able to break through. So the decision was made to send a platoon by a roundabout route, by way of Beit Shemesh. Before their departure the

---

116 Uncle Judah served in the Haganah and fought at Latrun, some of the most difficult (and unsuccessful) battles of the war. He wrote a wonderful collection of poems based upon his experiences called, *Jerusalem Has Many Faces*.
117 This was a block (*gush*) of four Jewish settlements located in a strategic area south of Jerusalem: Kfar Etzion, Masuot Yitzchik, Ein Tzurim and Revadim. All four settlements fell in the War of Independence. 240 people were killed and another 260 were taken captive. http://www.gush-etzion.org.il/history.asp. My father's cousin Esther, daughter of Rivka Stampfer Ben-Arieh, married Yitzchak Mivzari, who had been one of the original members of the religious kibbutz Ein Tzurim in the gush. The survivors reestablished the kibbutz on land near Ashkelon and we shared many wonderful *shabbatot* with the Mivtzaris there. After the 1967 war the *Gush* was rebuilt, including a new *kibbutz* now named Rosh Tzurim.

commander, Danny Mas, asked the soldiers, "Who is married?" Joshua, who was already married, raised his hand and was left behind.[118] The platoon went on their way from the Hartov settlement. About five kilometers before Gush Etzion, between the Arab villages of Geva and Tzorif, the platoon was discovered by two Arab women who alerted the Arabs of the nearby village. The battle that ensued lasted several hours. All 35 members of the platoon were killed, every single one.[119]

My Sister Pesha

Pesha, like all my sisters, was a wise and goodhearted woman. She accompanied Abba on his trip to India in 1935, when he was invited to serve as an expert witness in the court arbitration already described. She was married to Shlomo Altman, the son of the rabbi from Ekron, and they had two sons: Yehudah and David. Pesha died of cancer at an early age.

My Sister Rachel

Rachel married Yisrael Kaplan, an energetic and free thinking immigrant from Poland.[120] They met in Tel Aviv and

---

[118] My father's memory is that the commander told him that he wasn't seasoned enough for the strenuous hike with a heavy backpack and he was instructed to remain behind. This brush with death had a profound impact on my father, inspiring him to work hard to make contributions to the Jewish people—which he and my mother did through their own family of five children and many Jewish instutions in the Pacific Northwest of the United States.

[119] This is a well known story in Israel. There are streets named Ha-Lamed Heh (the 35) and a kibbutz called Netiv Ha-Lamed Heh (the pathway of the 35), which was built at a spot along the route they took. We used to pass by it on the road from Jerusalem to Tel Aviv in 1966 (the round about road that existed before the Six Day War)—unmistakable because of its large swimming pool, a rarity in those days. I'd always wonder what Dad thought when we passed it. He had been relatively new to the platoon, so he didn't have a strong personal connection with those who died, but even so ...

[120] Dodah Rachel and Kaplan (it was a long time before I even knew he had a first name!) were very important figures in our lives. My grandmother deeply missed

wanted to married, but the young immigrant had no money, no dowry and no dependable income. My mother, who was the practical one in the family and the one who made things happen, came to his aid and put together a dowry for them. With the money he received, Yisrael bought German machines and in 1935 opened a spring factory in Tel Aviv. This was before World War II and the business prospered. They moved from their home in Tel Aviv to a large house which they built in Ramat Gan and continued to welcome guests with their usual hospitality. They had four sons: Avner, Yossi, Amiram and Yehonatan.

Rachel was a one of a kind personality. Friends and family used to visit her home and everyone loved her and admired her. These guests included Aharon and Chava Verba, who visited with their young daughter, who is currently the head of the supreme court, Justice Doris Beinish. Bat-Ami and Shimon Finkel, who was actors at Habima, were also guests, and many many others.

---

her family when they moved to the U.S. and in 1929 my grandfather arranged for her and their two sons to spend the year in Israel. My father often remarks upon his father's self-sacrifice in making this happen. My grandmother, father and uncle all lived with Dodah Rachel in Tel Aviv. I have the vaguest baby memories of visiting the family in Ramat Gan when I was four years old, but the impressions were of a warm, lively and extremely loving woman.

Rachel and Yisrael Kaplan, with their four sons: Avner, Yossi, Amiram and Yehonatan, Ramat Gan 1950.

Avner, the first born son of the Kaplan family, was drafted into the paratroopers. He was wounded in the Sinai Campaign, recovered from his wounds and joined a Nachal *gareen* (literally, "seed," an army group that would also settle the land) The *gareen* was sent to Kibbutz Tel Katzir, a frontier settlement on the Syrian border, on the south-eastern shore of the Kinneret. An accident occurred during a Purim party on the *kibbutz*, a fire broke out and Avner, who was wearing a flammable costume, was badly burned and was taken to the hospital in critical condition. For weeks he suffered great pain and teetered between life and death, and in spring of 1959 he passed away, a precious young man just in his 20's.

His death literally broke my sister. She became ill and died a short time later.[121] The three sons she left behind

---

[121] Although Avner's death did indeed break my aunt, she did not die until a few years later, in 1963.

became paratroopers, just like their brother. The second son, Yossi, completed an officer training course, reached the rank of major, and during the Six Day War fought with his platoon reaching the Suez Canal; Amiram served in the 55th brigade, which fought the battle to liberate Jerusalem; and Yehonatan fought in the Golan Heights and was decorated for his role in the battle.

After the Six Day War Yossi was sent on a secret mission in Iran, whose main purpose was to train Kurdish fighters, led by Mustafa Barzani, against the Iraqi government. He was even invited to the palace of the Shah, in celebrating the anniversary of the Persian monarchy.[122] When he returned home to Israel he sought a discharge from the army, but the commander of the Bik'a Brigade Moshe Levi, who was known by the nickname, "Moshe-and-a-half," and who later became the 12th commander in chief of Tzahal, asked him to remain in the army and serve in the Bik'a (the Jordan valley), which was then known as the "Land of the Pursuers." Yossi agreed. His unit dealt with pursuing terrorist infiltrators and after four months, during an encounter with terrorists, Yossi was killed along with two friends, Channan Samson and Boaz Sasson. Their deaths caused great waves, for it emerged afterwards that they had compassion on a nursing mother sitting in the mouth of a cave. She sheltered a terrorist who was hiding in the cave who shot at the three soldiers at close range and killed them. He was only 27 years old when he died.[123]

---

[122] In October, 1971, the Shah of Iran hosted a spectacular celebration of 2500 years of the Persian Monarchy (although, as the New York Times, notes, the Shah himself was not of regal lineage—he was the son of a peasant. NY Times 10/14/1971). Seven years later the Shah and his family had to flee the country in the face of a revolution.

[123] In 1967 we were living in Nayot, a neighborhood in Jerusalem very close to the Valley of the Cross. Yossi came to Jerusalem for Israel Independence Day to participate in the military parade, and visited us. He was an extremely warm

GOODNESS AND MERCY SHALL FOLLOW ME

On the government memorial page of the Ministry of Defense, it is written among other things:

Yossi Kaplan, the son of Israel and Rachel. Born on the 24th of Nissan 5702 (4/11/1942) in Jerusalem. Yosef studied in the Hamatmid Elementary School in Ramat Gan and after a year, decided to enroll in the military boarding school of the Riali School in Haifa ... After completing his studies

and lively person who instantly drew people to him. We don't know a whole lot about his army service, since so much of it was classified. But I do remember that my father visited Israel sometime in the late 1968 and got a ride from Haifa to Tel Aviv with Kaplan. My dad said that his driving was worse than usual (!) and when my dad asked what was going on, Kaplan said that Yossi was participating in a special mission, but he didn't know the details. The next day my dad heard about a raid on the Beirut Airport where elite members from the IDF blew up empty planes in retaliation for a hijacking of an El Al plane earlier that year. Yossi's death was devastating to us all. We got a phone call from Israel—no small thing in 1969. My dad wasn't home at the time, and my mother asked our friend, Rabbi Solomon, who was visiting from Vancouver, to break the news. It was the first time I witnessed someone giving terrible news and one of the few times I saw my father cry.

in the military boarding school he was drafted into Tzahal in September, 1961, and volunteered for the paratroopers, in the footsteps of his older brother (who was killed two years earlier in Tel Katzir. He too had been a paratrooper and left a type of "testament" to his brothers that if they don't fulfill his mission in Nachal, they should volunteer for paratroopers). Yosef went to a company commander course and one year later was sent to an officer training course. Upon completing the course as a departmental outstanding student, he returned to the paratroopers and advanced in the levels of commander, until he become the commander of a company, attaining the rank of major.

In this role he commanded a company during the Six Day War in the Sinai battles, and afterwards he was transferred to an elite unit in Tzahal and from there he was transferred to an officer in the operational department in a paratrooper unit. He was considered an outstanding officer and a brave soldier, and was an outstanding friend. As a unit commander he maintained the discipline in his unit ... his regard for the soldiers and the regard the soldiers held toward him was extremely high. He was admired by those he commanded for his humanity... one friend emphasized Yosef's quietness, which flowed from his internal confidence; whatever he wanted to say was said quietly, concisely, clearly and with a confident voice. While serving in the Bik'a he encountered terrorists and during the battle and pursuit that took place on the 21st of Adar 5729 (3/11/1969), he died. He was brought to eternal rest on the military cemetery in Kiryat Shaul.[124]

---

[124] The death of these three soldiers—Yossi was shot while coming to the aid of a wounded comrade—caused shock waves in Israel and unleashed a public debate about the decision not to disturb the nursing mother at the mouth of the cave where terrorists were hidden, and the limitations of military ethics.

NOT MUCH LATER, AFTER THE DEATHS OF TWO OF HIS sons and his wife, Yisrael Kaplan, husband of my sister, Rachel, died of a broken heart.[125]

But this was not the end of the family's suffering. The youngest son, Yehonatan, was recruited into the *Mossad* (secret service) after his army service and was in Europe when the Yom Kippur War broke out.[126] When he learned of what was taking place on the front he pulled every string in order to return to Israel. Immediately upon his return he joined his paratrooper buddies fighting on the Egyptian front.[127] Yehonatan fought in the Sinai war front and the western side of the Suez Canal, and was killed in battle there. He was only 28 years old when he died. In the official memorial page of Yizkor, it is written, among other things:

---

125 Kaplan, upon hearing of Yossi's death, had a heart attack and suffered subsequent heart attacks every year on Yossi's yahrzeit. In the summer of 1973, just a few months before the outbreak of the Yom Kippur War, he underwent open heart surgery and died on the operating table. He literally died of a broken heart.
126 Yonatan was a brother to us. In 1962 my parents invited him to live with us for a year—our own foreign exchange program. He brought a whole new level of energy to cheering on the Lincoln High School basketball games and his driving instructor never quite recovered from the experience of his first Israeli student. We all loved him quite deeply. My son and my great-nephew are named for him.
127 When the war broke out we were all relieved to know that Yonatan was in Rome. We didn't know he had returned to Israel until Dodah Esther called us with the devastating news.

Yehonatan Kaplan, son of Rachel and Yisrael z"l, was born on the 15th of Tevet 5706 (12/19/1945) in Tel Aviv. He was the fourth son of the Kaplan family, whose roots were deeply planted in Eretz Yisrael. He studied in the Hamatmid Elementary school and continued his studies at the Dvir High School in Ramat Gan. In 1962 he went to the United States and completed high school in Portland, Oregon. Yoni was the youngest of the four brothers in the family and therefore he always wanted to catch up with them and be their equal. Despite this there was never any competition between the brothers due to jealousy. They very much loved one another, helped one another, and shared everything they had. Joy, happiness, and an optimistic approach to life were the primary characteristics of Yoni's personality.

It wasn't just that he was full of *joie de vivre*, but all of his being radiated joy and warm heartedness, which attracted everyone who came within his presence ... There was a very special relationship between Yoni and Yossi, the second brother, who died in pursuit of a ring of terrorists in the Jordan valley. There were many similarities between Yossi and Yoni's personalities. After his brother's death Yoni saw himself as the one to carry out his brother's life, and in many ways he followed his footsteps and his dreams ... Within his soul was a mixture of the innocence of youth along with wisdom and maturity, the rough edges of adolescence along with much charm and tenderness. Many people loved this unusual combination, which gave his character such fascinating complexity .... Yehonatan joined Tzahal in August, 1964 and volunteered to serve as a paratrooper. After basic training, and a course in parachuting, he continued on and completed explosives training. He was an outstanding soldier, who knew how to best use the weapons and men at his disposal. His commanders quickly recognized his many talents and made sure to move him up the ranks rapidly. After a commanders course he was sent to an officer training course for the infantry. He completed these two courses with great success. The soldiers who served under his command loved him and trusted his ability to lead them. In their annual officer evaluations, his commanders noted his seriousness and quick thinking. They considered him a strict officer, disciplined and responsible. He was willing to do any assignment and was fully prepared to execute any mission given to him. His knowledge in the field of explosives and the rest of infantry skills was comprehensive and he won much praise for his achievements. Despite his great success in his military work, he never saw his future within that framework. After his discharge he enrolled at Tel

Aviv University and began to study economics and political science. Afterwards he worked in the office of the prime minister in a classified capacity, and within this context he was sent on a mission outside of Israel in 1971. He achieved success in this work as well, and was appreciated by his superiors. During the Yom Kippur War Yoni participated in the hard and bitter battles on the Sinai front, and on the western side of the Suez Canal. He commanded an explosives platoon in the engineering company of a paratrooper's brigade. On the 24th of Tishrei 5734 (10/20/1973) he died of wounds received while directing a force that fought on the northern ramp of the canal. He was laid to rest in the Kiryat Shaul cemetery, buried next to his brother, Yossi.

THE KAPLANS, A WARM, HAPPY AND LIVELY FAMILY OF six, paid the price of living in the land with their own lifeblood. Let their memories be a blessing. The heart refuses to accept the tragedy, especially the deaths of the three young men who weren't able to establish families and died in their youth. Amiram, whose loved ones departed within such a short period of time, is the only one who remains, the sole survivor of the Kaplan Family.[128]

MY SISTER MINAH

Minah married Rabbi Grunnem Lando, a true scholar. After they married they moved to the United States and lived there for about 10 years, before returning to Israel. They had three sons: Yehudah, David and Danny. She died in 2001 at a ripe old age. Let their memories be a blessing.

---

128 We have home movies that my parents took in 1947, including visits to the Kaplan's lovely and hospitable home in Ramat Gan. It breaks your heart.

My Brother Yaakov

My brother Yaakov, seven years my senior (born in 1910) lived a turbulent and mysterious life. There were many times when he took his life in his hands and at least twice he had a close brush with death. In 1929 Yaakov was a student in the Hevron Yeshiva and was saved from the massacre in Hevron by heeding Imma's request that he return home to take part in a family celebration.

Yaakov joined the Haganah at a young age. In 1938, when Arabs governed over the Temple Mount and a large portion of Jerusalem, Harold McMichael, the high commissioner, ordered that "natives" may not be included in restoring peace to its place. However, the British police needed guides and trackers. Yaakov, who had connections with the British, was summoned to headquarters so he could lead the soldiers of His Royal Majesty through the alleyways of Jerusalem. The Arabs were aware of Yaakov's activities and began to look for *Ibn-Chakim*, (son of the rabbi). Haganah men came to our house to warn us that the Arabs were looking for Yaakov, so Imma decided that he needed to go to America until their anger passed. The American consul demanded a letter of consent from Abba, and when Abba gave his consent, Yaakov went to America.

When he arrived in New York he joined the American Army and joined the Fourth Division, which fought in Japan and in the Philippines. He was wounded in battle and returned to New York.

In 1946 in New York Yaakov met Yaakov Dori, who later became the first commander in chief of Tzahal. At that time Dori was involved with purchasing boats for illegal immigrants. He acquired five ships, but lacked a crew. My brother recruited dozens of young Jewish men who sailed on the ships from America to Europe. They picked up refugees and then continued to the shores of Israel.[129] My brother went out on such missions several times, and was involved in preparing and staffing the crews of the ships, "Haganah," "Biriya," "Ha-Chayal Ha-Ivri," and "Josiah Wedgewood." "Wedgewood" was purchased by the Institute for Aliyah Bet (illegal immigration) in Quebec, Canada.[130] On the 19th of June, 1946, the ship departed from a remote port in Italy; it carried 1,257 refugees, most of them European Holocaust survivors. After sailing for six days a British plane appeared in the sky and located the boat—followed by two British destroyers. The refugees resisted passively, the ship was towed to the Port of Haifa, and the refugees were transferred to the Atlit Camp and released after two weeks. The crew, however, including my brother Yaakov, received orders to break out detention and managed to escape in the confusion that erupted in the port. There was a curfew in Jerusalem, so Yaakov couldn't come home. So, without advance warning and as a complete surprise, my brother, Yaakov, arrived at our home in Petach Tikva. It goes without saying that there was a great deal of excitement.

---

129 The story of Machal, *Mitnadvei Chutz La'Aretz*, (volunteers from abroad) is a fascinating one. Approximately 1500 volunteers from United States and Canada, Jews and Christians, stepped up to help bring refugees to Israel in defiance of the British blockade. They also helped arrange arms aquisitions and smuggling operations. Forty of these volunteers gave their lives in this effort. The archives and a museum are located at the University of Florida, Gainesville. http://israel-vets.com/home.html

130 *Aliyah Bet*—the clandestine immigration movement, began in Eretz Yisrael—actually began in 1937. There were 62 voyages of refugees from Europe to Israel between 1937 and 1944. Many lives were lost at sea. After World War II ended, the activities of *Aliyah Bet* increased. The *Briha* ("Flight") network, helped Holocaust survivors, displaced persons, move from the Russian controlled zone to the American controlled zone, and from there attempts were made to bring them to Israel. Over 90% of the ships were intercepted by the British and by 1948 over 50,000 Jewish refugees were held in internment camps in Cyprus. http://www.ushmm.org/wlc/en/article.php?ModuleId=10005776

During the War of Independence my brother served as a lieutenant commander of the Givati brigade. He knew English and gained much military experience in the American army.[131] He did not remain long with Givati, however. Aharon Remez, who later became the second commander of the air force, who already knew Yaakov from the Haganah, and was impressed with him, took him to help organize the Israeli air force, which was then taking its first steps. Remez was then named as operations officer for the "Air Service," and within the framework of this job he dealt with acquiring and preparing British army bases in Israel for the use of the Israeli air force.

When the War of Independence ended and Yaakov was released from the army, he joined me as a partner in running the spring factory. One day he announced that he had to go abroad, and gave no details. It turned out that it was a governmental mission, and he went under an assumed name, Ismail Tishbach, to bring Iraqi Jews to Israel in an operation called "Ezra and Nehemiah." The operation began in 1950 and flew more than 120,000 Iraqi Jews to Israel. The operation ended in July, 1951.[132]

---

[131] Dod Yaakov was the easiest relative to converse with because his English was so good and so American. He never rolled his "R's." He was already in the States when my grandmother died. He was the one who broke the news to my father, who had just started his studies at the University of Chicago, and accompanied my dad back to Akron. My father recalls that one of the reasons that Dod Yaakov joined the United States Army was his thought that he could make his way back to the Middle East via Europe. Instead, he was sent to the Pacific. He was wounded in action and received a Purple Heart. In the mid-seventies he served as a member of the Israeli Knesset as part of the labor coalition.

[132] In 1948 there were about 135,000 Jews in Iraq, about half of them in Baghdad. Iraq participated in the war against the fledgling State of Israel and was the only Arab country that did not sign on the cease fire which ended that war. In 1948 the Iraqi government arrested thousands of Iraqi Jews on suspicion of involvement in Zionist activities. Jews faced many restrictions, including emigration to Israel. In 1950 the government took an about face and permitted Iraqi Jews to leave, although they had to relinquish their citizenship, their property and any right of return. During Operation Ezra and Nehemiah most of the Jewish population of Iraq came to Israel. www.moia.gov.il/Moia_en/AboutIsrael/

Yaakov married only at the age of 50. Abba never pressed him to get married; He did not want to cause him to transgress the commandment of honoring your father and mother. But from time to time Abba would say to me, "Tell him, urge him to find a wife, that he should get married already!" A year after Abba died, Yaakov married Mina of the Abramson family, one of the founders of the Moshava Kinneret and widow of the pilot Modi Alon. Their son, Zvi Frank, named for Abba, served as a pilot in the air force and is today a businessman.[133] My brother Yaakov died in 1993. May his memory be a blessing.

THE PILOT MODI ALON, THE FIRST HUSBAND OF MY sister-in-law Mina, commanded the first combat flights in the air force. During the War of Independence Egyptian Dakota aircraft bombed Tel Aviv with almost no interference. On the evening of June 3, 1948, when two Egyptian Dakota aircraft appeared again the skies over the city, Modi Alon took off to challenge them in his Messerschmitt. A dog fight took place right above the main streets of the city. The residents, who heard the bursts of fire left their shelters, and watched what was going on from the rooftops. One of them even immortalized the moment with his camera. Modi damaged the first plane, which quickly lost altitude and crashed on the beach south of Bat Yam. The second plane tried to get away, and pursuit took place, ending in the skies over Nes Tziyona/Rechovot. The Egyptian pilot looked for appropriate targets to drop his bombs, but Modi trailed him and managed to hit the Dakota with a few pre-

ezraVenechmia.htm. An interesting (and sad) memoir on this subject is *My Father's Paradise: A Son's Search For His Jewish Past in Kurdish Iraq*, by Ariel Sabar.
133 Zvika is my father's youngest first cousin—they are about 40 years apart in age.

cise shots. The Dakota dove and crashed on the beach west of Rechovot. It was said that in Samuel Square in Tel Aviv people were dancing and that Modi's room was flooded with bouquets of flowers, packages of chocolate and bottles of champagne—gifts from the citizens of Tel Aviv.

Around five months later, on the 13th of Tishrei 5709 (October 16, 1948), Modi Alon died. He returned from an aerial attack in Ashdod, his plane was damaged and crash landed. Modi Alon was buried in the military cemetery in Nachalat Yitzchak. His wife, Mina, was pregnant, and his daughter, Michal, was born a few months after his death. Twelve years after his death, Modi Alon's widow was married a second time to my brother Yaakov.

My Brother Yehudah

In 1930 my brother Yehudah went to learn in the Telz Yeshiva in Lithuania. There he became friendly with a great learner, who had a vast memory, by the name of Mottel Pargamanski. Students used to turn to Mottel with different questions and he'd immediately direct them without looking into books, to the right page of the Gemara. He knew entire books by heart.

Mottel Pargamanski arrived at the *yeshiva* at a relatively mature age. He told my brother that in his youth he had been a merchant, importing from Germany and selling in Poland and Lithuania. During one of his travels he spent a night in a hostel near Kovno, where he met a Jew by the name of Rabbi Eliyahu Lupian, one of the great Mussar teachers, who later became the spiritual advisor in Kfar Chassidim and the *yeshiva* "Knesset Hizkiyahu" in Ruchsin. They got into a conversation and Rabbi Eliyahu asked him:

"How is it that such an intelligent Jew such as yourself is not learning in *yeshiva*?" "Simple. They never sent me to learn," answered Mottel Pargamanski.

Rabbi Eliyahu Lupian continued to take an interest in the young man and learned that standing before him was the grandson of a scholar from the city of Yanov, in the Lublin district of Poland. He suggested that he learn in the Kelem yeshiva and gave him a letter of recommendation. The studies fascinated Pargamanski and a short time later he sold off his business and moved from the Kelem Yeshiva to the Telz Yeshiva, where he met my brother.

And now an interesting story. In 1941 the Nazis captured Lithuania and its neighbors and continued eastward. Mottel Pargamanski had made his way to the terrible Kovno ghetto. One night he was walking near the fence surrounding the ghetto when he suddenly heard a voice outside calling, "Are you Mottel Pargamanski?"

"Yes," he answered, "and who are you?"

"I can't tell you, but I've been ordered to rescue you," said the voice in the darkness. "Meet me at the same place tomorrow at the same time and I will get you out."

The next day the stranger arrived armed with wire cutters. He cut the fence and got Mottel Pargamanski out from the ghetto. "Who are you?" Mottel asked his rescuer. It turned out that he was a Jew married to a non-Jew who was living under an assumed name, and no one in the area knew his origins. He said that his father had appeared to him in a dream and said to him: "In the Kovno Ghetto there is a precious Jew by the name of Mottel Pargamanski, and you must save him!" The Jew continued, "I woke up and told myself that it was only a dream and went back to sleep. The next night my father again appeared in my dream, said the same thing and was even more specific, saying that you stroll at night in the ghetto in the vicinity that I met you. I tried again to dismiss the dream and forget these things, but father returned every night for a week and even added: 'I will haunt you until you save him!'"

The Jew did what his father commanded. He hid Mottel in a secure location, brought him food and protected him until the war ended. Afterwards he sent him to recover in Switzerland. But, tragically, Mottel was already mortally ill and died there. He told the strange and uncanny story of his rescue to Holocaust survivors on their way to Israel, while lying on his deathbed. After his death, Mottel Pargamanski was buried in Bnai Brak. My brother, Yehudah, took part in the burial and paid his final respects.

Yehudah learned at the Telz Yeshiva for two years. After that he transferred to the Mir Yeshiva in Poland, and returned to Israel two years later. He married Yehudit Berman and they had three children: Nechama, Yisrael and Chava. Yehudah became a businessman and died in 2004.

My Sister Esther[134]

My younger sister Esther took care of Abba for about 17 years, until his dying day, selflessly and with care that defies description. In the summer of 1943 Esther was in her eighth month of pregnancy. One evening her husband, Rabbi Shmuel Rozovsky, one of the heads of the Ponevitch Yeshiva in Bnai Brak, went to Jerusalem and she came to stay

---

[134] Dodah Esther was an amazing person, brilliant, elegant and charming, a legendary cook and hostess. She was one of the very few of our Israeli relatives who visited us in Portland. She had a great curiosity about the world, read voraciously and was capable of handling any situation. She had a regal bearing and I have many happy memories of sitting in her kitchen, sipping tea, chatting and watching her work her magic with pots, pans and the stove.

with our sister Rachel in Tel Aviv, where I was also living at the time. That same evening I was informed that Imma's condition had worsened. I didn't say a word to Rachel or Esther, so as not to worry them, and I left immediately for Jerusalem. The Egged bus was not running at that time of night, so I went to Jaffa first and then took an Arab taxi for Jerusalem. I arrived at my parent's home around 8 p.m. The family members huddled worriedly in the house and Imma was lying on her deathbed, but she was still concerned about us all: "Look, Avraham, I've had a bad day and there are a lot of people in the house. Please make sure that they all have something to eat." I prepared a salad, cooked up something, invited everyone to come and eat and then I went to sit beside Imma's bed. She burned with fever and had trouble breathing, but was as clear thinking as ever. She spoke with me about Esther's upcoming childbirth and said: "If Esther has a son there will be a *brit milah*, and guests will come. I'm not sure that I'll be up to it." And with that, with tranquility and peacefulness, she turned her head towards the wall and passed away.

Stricken with anguish and sorrow, I returned to my sister Rachel's house along with Shmuel Rozovsky, Esther's husband. Abba feared that given the advanced stage of Esther's pregnancy she might collapse and asked us not to tell her the bitter news and just tell her that the situation was critical. So, when we arrived at Rachel's house I wore work clothes so that my sisters would think that I was going to the plant, and Esther's husband said to her, "I'm tired. We didn't sleep all night. Let's go home." They took a taxi to Bnai Brak. Then I took off my work clothes and put on proper clothes, and told Rachel that we have to go to Jerusalem. As we approached the city Rachel said, "I want to go directly to the hospital." "There's no more reason to go there," I told her and she covered her face with her hands and cried.

A large crowed accompanied Imma on her final journey. When Abba spoke about her many people had a difficult time controlling their tears. We told Esther about Imma's death only towards the end of the *shiva* week. On the 30th day (marking the end of the *sheloshim* period of mourning) after Imma's death Esther gave birth to a daughter, who was named Gitah Malkah, for her grandmother. Afterwards Esther had a son and then two daughters: Michel David, Sarah and Ella.[135]

After Imma's death Esther took upon herself the running of the household and helped Abba with everything. She was true to the tradition, heart and soul, a wise woman like Imma, faithful, intelligent and clever.

My Brother Feivel

Feivel, my parents' youngest child, married Chaya Braverman, from Petach Tikva. He established a large factory for medical cotton. He had three sons and a daughter: Baruch, Tanchum, Dov and Gitah Malkah. He had a beautiful voice and more than anything else I loved to hear him read the Torah on Rosh Hashanah and on Yom Kippur. Tragically, Feivel died at a young age from a serious illness.

---

[135] Dod Avram chose to leave out the fact that Dodah Esther and Shmuel Rozovsky divorced, which also leaves out a poignant story that deserves to be told. When Shmuel Rozovsky developed lung cancer in 1978 he come to Boston for treatment. Dodah Esther wanted to be there with him and help him, but it would have been inappropriate if they were unmarried, so they remarried. He died a few months later.

Chapter Nine

My Uncle, Rabbi Aryeh Levin

Rabbi Aryeh Levin was my uncle, the husband of Channah Tziporrah, my mother's sister. He was born in 1885 in Orla, near Bialystok in White Russia. He learned at the Slotzk, Slonim and Volozhin yeshivas and arrived in Jaffa in 1905 as a young man of 24. There was no Absorption Office, or Aliyah Department nor Jewish Agency then. Instead there were a few charitable groups and individuals who helped the new immigrants. Among them was Reb Moshe Betzalel, who also helped my father when he arrived in Israel. As was his usual practice, Reb Moshe Betzalel invited the young man to eat in his house, hosted him for about two weeks, was impressed with the young man and suggested that he go learn in Jerusalem. He provided him with a letter to Rabbi Frank and asked that he welcome him. My father, of course, welcomed the young man with proper respect, introduced him into the Torat Chayim Yeshiva and invited him home for Shabbat. That is how Aryeh Levin met Channah Tziporrah, Imma's sister, whom he married.

Rabbi Aryeh Levin was ordained by Rabbi Shmuel Salant, Rabbi Kook and Rabbi Chayim Berlin (the son of the head of the Volozhin Yeshiva who was the rabbi of Moscow before immigrating to Israel). He began to work as a spiritual counselor at the Etz Chayim Yeshiva, considered to be one of the best Talmud Torahs in the country. He showered endless devotion, love and care upon the children. He once met a lad crying in the street, and even though he didn't know him he succeeded in coaxing the child to speak with him, and it turned out that, in great distress, the boy had run away from an orphanage. Reb Aryeh persuaded the boy to return to the orphanage and promised that he would take responsibility for him, that from now on he and his household would be his adoptive family. And that's what happened.

Reb Aryeh used to regularly visit the hospital for lepers in Jerusalem, something then considered to be a serious act of self-sacrifice because of the fear of contracting the disease. Every Friday he would check with the head nurse to find out which patients had no visitors and that's where he would begin his visits. He aided the patients and helped them with every fiber of his being.

With the outbreaks of the riots in 1929 and then in 1936, the British incarcerated Jewish members of the underground, Haganah, Etzel and Lechi, and Reb Aryeh made it his habit to visit them in prison. That's how he became known as the "Rabbi of the Underground Prisoners." Every Shabbat Reb Aryeh would pray with the prisoners, and encourage them by saying, "I am jealous of your strong spirit," and he called them "angels." Rabbi Aryeh Levin wasn't able to bring the prisoners to freedom, but he brought the entire world to those trapped in their cells. He related to them like a father to his children, understanding the subtext of their words, creating happiness for them and bringing greetings to them from home. After the prayers he always tried to go around to their families and bring greetings from their loved ones. Even the imprisoned members of Haganah, Palmach and infantry, most of whom were kibbutz members, even from Hashomer ha-Tzair, honored and loved him. When Shabbat came the young men would put on their *kippot*, and went to meet him in order to hear his words of encouragement and love pouring upon them. They told me that the prisoners would not count the days of the week by their names, Monday, Tuesday etc., but rather, "First day after the rabbi's visit," "two days after the rabbi's visit," and so forth, until "one day before the rabbi's visit."

Geulah Cohen, a former member of parliament, radio announcer for Lechi, who was imprisoned in 1946 in Bethlehem, told of Reb Aryeh's visits. According to her, his visits raised the spirits of the imprisoned women and inspired them with hope. He made them smile when he would clasp his hands together as an indication that it wasn't his custom to shake a woman's hand.

In 1944 Anshel Shpilman, a Lechi fighter, was sentenced to 10 years imprisonment. One day he secretly received a command to find a way to escape that week since they needed him to carry out an operation. Shpilman tried to escape, but didn't succeed. On Shabbat morning, when Reb Aryeh arrived at the prison, he approached Shpilman and whispered, "What?! You're still here?" Shpilman was shocked. It never occurred to him that anyone other than himself knew anything about the escape. Within a few weeks Shpilman succeeded in fulfilling his mission.

Motti Shmuelovitz, a Lechi man, was sentenced to death by the British. One night Rabbi Levin was summoned to recite the confession with him. When he left Shmuelovitz's cell he announced to the British commander: "Prepare two gallows." The commander was taken aback: "Who is the second one for?" "For me," the rabbi answered, "I can't stand on the side and watch a Jew hanged." The officer was impressed by the selflessness and delayed the hanging. Shmuelovitz was transferred to the famous Acco prison, and was freed from that place when the British Mandate ended. At three in the morning Reb Aryeh came to my father, who was still engrossed in his learning. Very much moved he told how he managed to save Shmuelovitz's life.

When Reb Aryeh reached his 80th birthday the mayor of Jerusalem implored him to accept the title of "Honored Citizen" from the city, but he refused. He lived modestly, never taking anything for himself. He was exceedingly humble and fled from honor. Reb Aryeh's son-in-law, Rabbi Yosef Shalom Elyashiv, said of him that if he could find one word to describe the essence of Reb Aryeh Levin, it would have to be "A genius of love and kindness."

My son-in-law, Dan Yardeni, told me a story about this precious man, which he heard from a cab driver who drove him when he (Reb Aryeh) was an elderly widower. The driver asked him where his home was, and he didn't answer. He asked again, but he still didn't answer. The driver got angry and asked "Where do you live?" and at that point Reb Aryeh gave him his address. When they reached the destination the driver asked the rabbi, "Why didn't you answer me the first time?" The elderly man said, "From the day my wife died I have no home, only an address."

In July, 2005, the 120th anniversary of the birth of Rabbi Aryeh Levin, and 100 years since his arrival in Israel, a governmental medallion was issued commemorating him. The sixth president of Israel, Chayim Herzog z"l wrote of him: This righteous man was blessed with unique characteristics of innocence and purity, of love of Israel and love for his fellow man with no restraints and without reckoning costs, of faith, warmth and a good heart. All of these radiated from him, from his person, his eyes, his gaze, his facial expressions. His words, which came from the heart, entered the heart, for they were words of truth and faith and not empty expressions. They were words of consolation and encouragement, words of healing and hope, words of love and gentle rebuke. Rabbi Aryeh Levin's heart and home were open to anyone who needed help, whether economic or spiritual. While he himself lived extremely modestly, he dedicated his time and income towards helping others and many came to his door, the leaders of the generation and the simplest folks as one.[136] More than anything else Rabbi Aryeh Levin's name has been distinguished and etched in the history of Israel as "The Prisoner's Rabbi," and especially when talking about the prisoners from the establishment of the state, the underground fighters. He did not come to them as a politician, since he never belonged to a faction or party of any kind. He was simply a complete Jew, who embodied in his personality all the integrity and purity that can exist in the human soul, and the unity of Israel radiated from him. He came to their aid in their time of distress, inspiring them with faith and identifying with their sublime sacrifice."

On the commemorative medallion issued in his memory, next to the shining face of the rabbi, a barred window is engraved, symbolizing the British prison and the sentence, "A Tzaddik In Our Time." On the other side, on the background of the neighborhood where he lived, "Mishkenot

---

[136] Unfortunately, people would take advantage of Rabbi Levin's kindness and my great-grandfather had to forbid him from co-signing loans. Raz, Simcha, *A Tzadik in Our Times*,translated and expanded by Charles Wengrov (Jerusalem: Feldheim, 1976), 114

Yisrael," the rabbi's hands are covered, in a characteristic gesture of support and comfort, by the hands of someone in need, and the blessing, "God's salvation comes in the twinkling of an eye," which he always said.[137]

The author Simcha Raz wrote two books about Reb Aryeh Levin: *A Tzaddik in Our Times*, and *The Righteous Is the Foundation of the World*, and his image continues to provide inspiration and encouragement in conducting the educational legacy of generosity and kindness.

---

137 A few summers ago I asked my father about his great-uncle, Reb Aryeh Levin. As soon as I said his name my dad's face utterly transformed and the most beautific smile spread across his face. I had never seen such a look on his face and it told me more about Reb Aryeh Levin than anything I have read. It had to have been at least 50 years since my father had been in Reb Aryeh's presence, but apparently his aura endured and was conveyed to me as well.

Bibliography

Agnon, Shai, *Tmol Shilshom* (Only Yesterday), Jerusalem: Shocken, 1946 (Heb.)

Ben Arieh, *Ir B' re'i Tekufah (A City As Seen Through an Era: Jerusalem in the 19th Century)*, Jerusalem Yad Yitzchak ben Zevi, 1977, (Heb)

Encyclopedia Judaica, Cecil Roth, editor. Jerusalem: Keter Publishing, 1972

Gilbert, Martin, *Israel, A History*. New York: William and Morrow Company, 1998.

Oz, Amos, *A Tale of Love and Darkness*, translated by Nicholas de Lange. Harcourt, Inc., 2003

Raz, Simcha, A *Tzadik in Our Times,* translated and expanded by Charles Wengrov. Jerusalem: Feldheim, 1976

Sachar, Howard, *A History of Israel,* New York: Albert Knopf, 1976

Stampfer, Shaul, *Families, Rabbis and Education: Traditional Jewish Society in Nineteenth-Century Eastern Europe*, Portland, Oregon: Littman Library of Jewish Civilization, 2010.

Tessler, Mark, *A History of the Israeli-Palestinian Conflict*, Indiana University Press, 1994

Tidhar, David, *Encyclopedia of the Founders and Builders of Israel*, 1947-1970 tidhar.tourolib.org (Heb.)

The Yivo Encyclopedia of Jews in Eastern Europe, Gershon David Hundert, Editor in Chief. Yale University Press, in Cooperation with the YIVO Institute for Jewish Research. 2008. (Heb.) Yivoencyclopedia.org

Websites
Aliyah Bet & Machal Virtual Museum: Israelvets.com

American-Israeli Cooperative Enterprise (AICE) Jewishvirtuallibrary.org
Circassian Research Group: Circassianworld.com
The Company for the Reconstruction and Development of the Jewish Quarter in the Old City of Jerusalem Ltd.: Jewishquarter.org.il
Gush Etzion Foundation: Gush-etzion.org.il
The Irgun Site, written by Prof. Yehuda Lapidot: Etzel.org.il
Ministry of Immigrant Absorption (State of Israel): Moia.gov.il
Museum of Jewish Heritage: Jewishgen.org
Official Website of Jerusalem: Jerusalem.muni.il
Official Website of Safed: Safed.co.il
Shaarei Zedek Medical Center: Szmc.org.il
JTA, The Global News Service of the Jewish People: Jta.org
The Jewish Encyclopedia, 1901-1906: Jewishencyclopedia.com
United States Holocaust Memorial Museum: Ushmm.com

In Honor of R' Avraham Frank

*By Supreme Court Justice
Elyakim Rubenstein*

Men of quality, from whom we can learn, live among us and aren't always the ones who appear on newspaper banner headlines; they are virtuous and humble and leave their mark through their approach towards life, their characteristics and way of living. They, in their modest way are the pillars of the well-ordered society. One such person is Avraham Frank, whose memories are the core of this book. His daughter and son-in-law did well to produce this book; this man should be known beyond the circle of his family and friends.

I got to know Avraham Frank about 10 years ago, when we moved to Palmach Street in Jerusalem, and I began to attend the weekday services at the well-established minyan at the "shtiblach" in Katamon [a nearby neighborhood] where Reb Avraham also prayed and I regularly sat by his side. On Friday nights I began to attend the Chazon Yehezkel Synagogue on Palmach Street, and I sat across from him. Immediately, despite the 30 year age gap—an entire generation—a certain chemistry developed, along with a great friendship. It wasn't just that R' Avraham safeguarded my seat for many years, since he was one of the first to arrive at the synagogue, but we had innumerable conversations and I learned much from him—about world views, the Zionist way of life, the history of Jerusalem and the Jewish population during the British Mandate and the early days of the State—through the lens of his many branched multi-generation family and his personal history, in terms of individuals and events.

R'Avraham Frank's life until now (may he live to 120), encompasses nine decades—from the time he was born within the walled city of Jerusalem in the waning days of the Ottoman Empire, through the British Mandate and sixty years of the State of Israel. He is a man full of charm and good humor, wise and possessing a phenomenal memory of details from the past as well as contemporary events. R' Avraham is a bona fide man of Israel [Eretz Yisraeli] and not only that, but there is something exemplary in the fact that, like the patriarch Isaac, he never left the Land of Israel to visit foreign places, living contentedly in the land. The focus is Jerusalem, even during the decades he lived elsewhere. He went from Jerusalem to learn in a yeshiva in Haifa in the early 1930's, from Jerusalem to the night patrol training of Wingate in the [Jezreel] Valley later in the 30's, from Jerusalem to Petach Tikva and Tel Aviv from the 40's to the 80's, and ending up in Jerusalem, where he began.

Above all, he is a branch of the land of his fore bearers. R'Avraham is proud of his paternal grandfather, one of the founders of Chadera, his maternal great great grandfather, the rabbi of Kovno, and, first and foremost, his father, the Gaon Rabbi Zvi Pesach Frank, ztz"l, the rabbi of Jerusalem. The son honors the father. R'Avraham does not presume to present himself as a Torah scholar. He honestly describes his memories in the Cheder and Yeshiva as a well-known mischief maker. Yet there are no limits to the honor he bears his father, which is intertwined with honoring Torah itself as it linked with his father—his father as a [halakhic] arbiter, his father as a judge, his father as a man of kindness towards *agunot*, his father as the wise unraveler of halachic complexities, strong minded, who feared no man, who understood the reality of the nation and the world, who looked with a keen eye at his children's activities in the struggle against the British, and decreeing legal leniencies in order to preserve lives of the Jewish population during the War of Independence. It is interesting to note in an historical and societal context which is unknown today, of a father and rabbi who was among the greatest of the great whose offspring spread out through the entire spectrum of society—Charedim, religious Zionists (including outstanding scholars), as well as members of the general society who are not identifiable by a *kippah*. His grandchildren and great-grandchildren included fearless fighters who died in defense of the homeland, as well as public figures of various types—if you like, in the synagogue and in the parliament (beit ha-knesset and the Knesset).

R'Avraham's father's name was ever present upon his lips and he loved to tell me stories about him. The late Gaon did not cease speaking of holy texts until his dying breath, as his son told me; books and publications about him continue to emerge today, five decades after his passing. So R'Avraham greatly rejoiced when his older brother Yehudah, before his death, managed to publish a long collection of letters that his father sent to him at the Telz Yeshiva in Lithuania in the early 1930's, while he [Yehudah] studied there. R'Avraham greatly honored his late mother who oversaw a large family of 15 children—of whom R'Avraham is the only one still alive, may he live long—and allowed her husband to immerse himself in Torah. R'Avraham was eternally in her debt, as well as to his sister, the Rabbanit

Esther Rozovsky, may she rest in peace, who, with boundless devotion, cared for her father for 17 years after the death of her mother.

R'Avraham was a physical presence, tall, broad shouldered, with a powerful bass voice that did not diminish over the years, up until today. That is how his childhood friends remember him, as do the children of the Bilu Synagogue in Tel Aviv. On the other hand, it would appear that there are those who remember his powerful arm towards rioting neighbors who tried to harm Jews during the struggle at the time of the Mandate. He once told me how he overcame six attackers in one such incident. My legal opinion is that it was self-defense, and, anyhow, it is beyond the statute of limitations.

I'll say one more word about R'Avraham's phenomenal memory. He recalls small details of the "Mishpachalogia" [family lore] of Jerusalem and its inhabitants in general, not just his own family—and this is no small matter when you consider the fact that his brother has great-great-grandchildren—but for many others as well. On more than one occasion he would point to someone on the street or the synagogue and tell me about his family. As to his own relatives—as he once told me, "How many people have 20 brothers-in-law?" (from his side and his wife's side). He was meticulous in attending not only celebrations, but, even more so, to memorials. In particular, the family plot on Har Hamenuchot and in other places, especially his three beloved nephews of the Kaplan family, two of whom were army casualties, when cruel fate cut their lives short while in the prime of life. But first and foremost the connection with the living was very important to him, including his many relatives in America, the descendants of his sisters, even though he never visited them, the connections were lively and long lasting, continuing over several generations. If he had any criticism regarding those relatives or others in Israel, they were "wounds by a loved one are long lasting" (Pr. 27:6). There were also sad incidents in his family that left their marks, but did not dampen his spirit. R'Avraham was also active in the Haganah and contributed to the security of Israel, through his spring factory, together with his brother (who was also a Haganah and IDF man, and active in public service), in R'Avraham's words "a factory himself." It becomes clear that he had an "additional soul" (neshamah yeterah) to be, on one hand, a steady supplier of the IDF and Defense Department and, on the other hand, an employer of Holocaust survivors, people struggling to get by and also at risk youth.

R'Avraham was proud of his activities in the synagogue associated with the Bilu School in Tel Aviv which was, in its time, a magnet for the city's religious youth, including the students at the school, plus the additional draw of the late Cantor Shlomo Ravitz and his choir. R'Avraham frequently described how the founding principal, the late Chaim Mishori, called to him from his deathbed, and placed upon him the responsibility of completing the holy ark, how he gathered funds, including his own contribution as well as convincing the contractor to contribute, until it was finally dedicated.

R'Avraham was a man of kindness and charity. Even though he was not among the wealthy, he wholeheartedly practiced the dictum, "Do not turn aside from your brother." Even with his own great acts of bravery he was keenly aware of all that transpired in the State and grieved over all who lost their lives in military actions or in terror attacks. He criticized the greater public policy, in terms of values as well as implementation, and worried deeply about the country's condition. His point of view was nationalistic and he clearly gave them voice.

His vitality did not diminish in the synagogue, As he begins the prayers with his booming voice, "That the temple be rebuilt speedily in our day and grant us our portion in your Torah, and There we will worship you with awe as was done in the ancient days," and when he calls out "Cohanim," to summon [the descendants of the priests] to pronounce the priestly blessing. His sense of humor emerges through convoluted stories. He loves history, sport (on television) and crossword puzzles. In short, it is hard to connect his biological age with his appearance and mental age, even when he complains of the aches and pains of old age. His wife, Malka, also a daughter of the early Yishuv in Jerusalem, Safed and even Shechem [Nablus], by his side for almost 63 years, is also wise, possessing a good sense of humor, and is a voracious reader. Their household excels—to this day—in hospitality and caring for others.

I will conclude with a blessing for the Frank couple, for good health, long life until 120, light from on high, and that they merit to continue to bring joy to God and people, enjoying satisfaction from their offspring.

By Rabbi David Hacohen,
Rosh Yeshiva of the Hevron Yeshiva, Jerusalem
Grandson of Tanchum, Avraham's oldest brother

Avraham is the foundation of the characteristic of kindness. Avraham is the foundation of the characteristic of love. "I have loved you with eternal love, therefore I have treated you kindly."

These words stand before me as I begin to write of memories and feelings to honor and praise the crown jewel of our family, our greatly beloved and admired R'Avraham Frank, for Avraham is the heart full and overflowing with love of God and people, and his heart contains a special chamber filled and overflowing with love for his family and loving relationships with each and every individual personally. Throughout his life he prioritized every matter that pertains to kindness to others in general, and in particular, and committed himself with all his heart and soul, towards those nearby and those far away.

I recall the long ago days, the great days when the home of great grandfather, the rabbi of Israel, stood firmly, and the house stood in its glory, endlessly spreading Torah and commitment towards the tribulations and troubles of each and every individual, serving as the central support for all kinds of support for the needy of Jerusalem. And I, as a young child, lived the life of that home with every fiber of my being, observing and absorbing its very soul, discerning and observing how each and every member of the household had his own place in the house and in its life. I am unable to forget the wonderful figure of the great uncle Avraham, who was a central figure in the house, the joy and liveliness that radiated and spread, the kindness and loving relationship he had with each individual he met, his eyes beaming and a boundless desire to give. Each time he arrived with his wonderful family, his well-mannered children, with whom I was bound with such loving ties, it was a holiday for us all and injected a special element to our family during the holidays and occasional shabbatot during the year.

All of the splendor of those days have been hidden away in the past and we are left with just a few fragments of memories from that wonderful era. But there can be no doubt that the final jewel of the house, may he live long, R'Avraham, is the thread that continues to attach us to the great home which nurtured us. By his merit we still have the connection and sense of belonging to those distant days. From time to time we still have the opportunity to listen to the memories and wonderful deeds from that period, and can briefly bring to mind those bygone days that still live within us.

A unique and unforgettable episode was when we experience the extended period of time, close to 20 years, during the illness of my mother and teacher, may her memory be a blessing, the daughter of R'Avraham's oldest brother, my righteous and upright grandfather Rabbi Tanchum Frank, may his memory be a blessing. Those were very difficult days for her and my late father, ztz"l. It is impossible to describe the hardships and difficulties that they endured during this time. The ray of light during those times were the visits of Uncle R'Avraham every Friday. He would stay in the house a few hours, straightening up and fixing all the things that needed attention. Any problem that came up in the house was deferred until Friday when Dod Avraham could take care of it. He lived the life of the household and its problems with all of his being. He participated wholeheartedly with each and every difficulty, advising, helping, encouraging, bringing a joyful spirit into a home full of sorrow and challenges. My mother, z"l, waited each week for his Friday visits and was reinvigorated with strength and courage for another week. We will never forget those days and we are full of gratitude towards him for all the kindness and goodness that he brought to our parents. May the good Lord repay him for all the deeds of kindness he performed and continues to do up until his old age with continued good health.

There are no words to express my feelings while writing this essay, nor am I able to describe the great character of Dod Avraham, but I cannot omit two central principles of his life. The first is his wonderful common sense. The years of his lifespan were, and still are, turbulent and fateful ones for the people of Israel. He endured the hardships and difficult battles that took placed before the state arose, followed by the difficulties surrounding the establishment of the state and the almost unceasing wars against the haters of Israel who rose up to destroy it. He took his place within the battle itself. His factory produced parts for armaments intended to protect from the enemy. He lived challenges and difficulties of the nation with all of his being, and gave wholeheartedly to help his people. During those stormy years he knew many leading individuals and saw much of motives behind man's deeds. He learned to distinguish and discern between truth and lies, between the honest and the false, and he could evaluate each person's work according to its true worth, and was also able to delve and analyze and recognize the nation's condition in general and in particular during each hour of that fateful period. His wonderful life wisdom allowed him to correctly assess the existing condition.

The second principle, which actually complements the first, was his simple and perfect faith in the Creator of the universe, the Rock of Israel and Redeemer, the Holy One Blessed be He. He believed with all his being that God would not withhold his kindness from his downtrodden people who were handed over to be plundered by the sword and to the hatred of the nations of the world. The complete faith that lived within him, that he would speedily merit to see the coming of our righteous messiah, this faith gave him the strength to continue along his true path to live a life of truth and integrity and to influence others with love and kindness.

It is impossible to conclude without a few words about the wonderful figure who stands by his side, the "queen" of the household [a play on words, since her name, Malka, means "queen"] who accompanies him with rare devotion and faithfulness. We all praise her and recognize her unstinting activities. We have much to learn from this wonderful couple, the way to live truthfully in a world of falsehood.

I can only conclude with the words of the priestly blessing [the author is himself a Kohen], with love to the dear aunt and uncle, that they may continue with their life work with good health until 120 years old, and that they receive much nachas [satisfaction and joy] from their wonderful family. May they continue to influence us all with their goodness, to faithfully join us at each and every celebration, as has been their practice all these years, and continue to be our final thread connecting us to the house of great grandfather until the true redeemer comes speedily to us.

Avraham Frank

*By Professor Shaul Stampfer, historian
Grandson of Nechama, Avraham's Sister*

The study of a person's life, as he narrates it, is a unique experience. On one hand, you have the life story of someone from his own perspective. He seeks to fulfil hopes and achievements, faces obstacles and impediments, and it is impossible not to feel emotion– to rejoice and sometimes to grieve. However, the life events of a person are also a portrait of an era. I particularly believe that an eyewitness can grasp things that one is unable to gather from scholarly and well documented research. We see this clearly in the narrative of Avraham Frank. This is true in regard to the individual perspective, and certainly in regard to the era. We speak of a man who has a unique personality, who accomplished a great deal in his life—and he did so by dint of his own efforts. His destiny was to be born in a unique time period. There is no era which is uninteresting, just as there is no era wherein great and small things don't take place. However, it would be difficult to identify eras that contain such extreme and weighty changes in the history of the Jewish people and the land of Israel as the generation that came before us.

Avraham Frank was born in the first years of the British Mandate in the land of Israel. There were few Jewish inhabitants at that time and there was little reason to expect any great change in their circumstances in the land of Israel. In those years the Jewish inhabitants in the land of Israel lived the traditional life of Jews outside the land, and spoke the traditional languages of Jews outside of Israel, be it Yiddish or Ladino or other languages. The Jews of the Old Yishuv, as well as the modern, knew the traditional Jewish community not from books and stories, but rather from lived experience. Along with this, willingly or unwillingly, they also were aware of the greater world around them. Even the most traditional Jews could not refrain from recognizing or even forging strong bonds with Arabs, with the secular, with scholars and with the most downtrodden. The generation has not yet been born who knows only those like themselves, who live in neighborhoods or areas where they have only anonymous contact with the "other." The years of the Mandate were years of continual change. We live in a generation today where it is a matter of course that children will generally grow up to be pretty much like their parents and will live in a world similar to their parents. Because of this the parents' experience allows them to be guides for their children. At the beginning of the 20th century this was not the case.

The generation of those born in the land during the years of the Mandate and the first few years of the State experienced a myriad of dramatic events. Many of these events and processes are mentioned here. The exit from the walls [of Jerusalem] was a multi-faceted exit, and not merely geographic. The balance of power shifted within the Jewish community and also between Jews and non-Jews. The process of building and expansion characterized the Jewish community. The struggle for the defense of the Jewish Yishuv took place simultaneously, as did the struggle for the hearts of the young generation. From Avraham's stories we learn that what may appear to be simple and obvious in hindsight, was completely different at the time.

It was easy in those days to be pulled to one extreme or another There were radical movements that advocated a complete revolution in Jewish life. There were also movements that claimed that one must resist every innovation on grounds of principle. Those two approaches were essentially totally new within the Jewish community and contradicted the tradition of Israel. But they held powerful attraction because they developed fundamental ideologies and because they were led by colorful and charismatic leaders. For that reason these movements and these leaders have attracted the attention of researchers and those who love to explore Jewish history. Much less attention has been given to those who quietly continued their ancestor's tradition of adaptation and renewal, harmonizing the story of Torah and earning a living, absorbing new ideas and still stubbornly standing in support of tradition, observing the laws of Israel while also being open to new publications. It was certainly possible to live a split life and on Saturday night to recite Havdalah, separating not only between the holiness [of Shabbat] to the secular [workday], but also separate between one world and another. However, there were also those who were pioneers in seeking to integrate and connect the old and the new. This was not a dramatic process, but it had greater importance than the divisive ideologies and the impact of this process continues to spread. In particular, this process is described here, especially if you look between the lines. Casual references allow one to reconstruct a process that few pay attention to.

There are many people who tell their life story and describe how they determined the fate of the nation or the state, or, at least, how they thought they caused those changes. There are also those who had some task in some important event and tell of their life—where the first part of their description is the preparation for that event and most of the latter part deals with the aftermath of the event. There is, of course, great interest in what is related in these stories, and the reader may conclude that they have learned from reading about them. However, this perusal may, of course, be deceptive and even greatly distorted. There is a long standing dispute whether historical processes are a result of the actions of great men or, perhaps, the determining causes are "fundamental" processes, such as economic or social factors that take place quietly, yet powerfully. There is no doubt that there is great importance attached to leaders' actions and great ramification to universal factors. However, everyone agrees that it is impossible to ignore the inner world of the thinking and feeling community who, in their actions and responses determined the destiny of leaders and social forces. The charm of the story told here lies in the fact that it sheds light on the life of this community—which was largely mute, but, despite this, important. Whereas others spoke, they acted. Without viewing this community, it is difficult to comprehend the shape of life in the land.

There is a unique quality to the description of the home of the Gaon Rabbi Zvi Pesach Frank. Many of the authors who write about the great ones of Israel do so because they belong to some institution, organization or movements that are connected to that great man. In their writings, they speak not only about the hero of their story, but also reveal something about themselves—about their importance as the ones continuing the way forward or as the explicators of the approach. This is especially true in regard to someone who heads an institution. Perhaps that is why so little has been written about Rabbi Zvi Pesach Frank, other than the wonderful biography written by R' Shabbetai Rosenthal. As far as I know, Rabbi Frank was never an institution man, and did not employ a community or staff. He was an exceedingly rare type of individual, a Torah scholar who dealt only in Torah and halakhic decisions. Therefore there is a dearth of written material about him. A person whose world is learning is rare indeed. It's more common to find the type who bemoans the fact that he is unable to focus on his learning—but he is quietly comfortable with that. It's much easier to integrate public activity, out of the purest of motives, with making halachic decisions. However, to devote oneself completely and wholly to Torah, ignoring the voices of those seeking to harness the scholar to their own political ends is rare. R' Frank was such a man and that is why there is only minimal preoccupation with him. However, this in no way diminishes from his importance in the world of Torah and Jewish law. On the contrary, it transforms him into an even greater figure—from whom we can learn and about whom we must learn. Actually, the image that emerges here about the family life of a great man is unique and important in light of the relative silence about his activities. In addition, describing a man who not only preached that one should engage in Torah study with no outside distractions challenge each one in his or her life to aspire to be upright and dedicated. This, however, sets an extremely high bar.

Each reader of Avraham Frank's life story will focus on different things and the readers' responses will certainly not be uniform. There is much in Avraham's story, much more than he even thinks. This is the story of an upright man who, instead of preaching, lived a life of integrity at home and outside his home. Avraham was successful in standing up for his views, but remains beloved by a range of people who represent a wide range of opinions—and he loves them in return. Here is a story of a remarkable family and a generation that underwent upheavals that are hard to imagine. The story is modest and to the point—much like the storyteller himself. However, we shouldn't read it without learning what lies behind what is stated explicitly, and it's worthwhile to pay attention to the implications for the present time. The life story of a man like this is not just an historical description, but it is also a book of ethics. The years of his life are the pages—and it is the reader who must supply the commentary—as well as to take care of the chapters to come.

And the Master of the House Draws Near to God

By Rabbi Shabbetai Rosenthal
Director, Har Zvi Institute, named for
Rabbi Zvi Pesach Frank

Our dear and beloved R'Avraham Frank is unique and special in the goodness of his heart and his generous qualities. As a native Jerusalemite he is outstanding in that he performs his deeds quietly and secretly without taking credit [ולא מחזיק טיבותא לנפשיה]. His good deeds are performed secretly without fanfare and the sounds of trumpets. As the Sages said, "Do things for its own sake and speak them in their own name. Do not make them a crown to adorn yourself and do use them as an axe to hoe with." (Nedarim 62a).

It is told that at the funeral of the Gaon Rabi Yehoshua Leib Diskin, the rabbi of Brisk, he was eulogized by the Gaon Rabbi Yitzchak Winograd, the head of the Torat Chayim Yeshiva. He said that of all the outstanding characteristics in which the patriarch Abraham excelled, he singled out the goodness of his heart, "And you found his heart to be faithful before You."

My father and teacher, Rabbi Yitzchak Rosenthal once mentioned that regarding the verse in the Book of Psalms, "God has given me a pure heart," (51:12) one should change the pronunciation regarding our R'Avraham, "God gave **him** a pure heart." Indeed, everyone points out his compassionate heart.

I will not recount here the many wonderful kindnesses he has performed. I hesitate because of Proverbs 27:14, "He who greets his fellow loudly early in the morning shall have it reckoned to him as a curse." He performs these deeds not in order to promote himself or to preen. He simply does them for their own sake, living Torah and loving kindness.

That being said, it is impossible to totally exempt myself. I know of a wonderful deed that he did which is completely unknown. His great grandfather, Rabbi Chaim Yaakov Shapira, the head of the rabbinical court of Jerusalem, had a young son, Rabbi Meshullam Zalman who died during his father's lifetime. His widow lived in Battei Horodna in the Machane Yehudah neighborhood, who supported herself with great suffering and deprivation, without any complaints or protests. The matter was known to her kinsman, the righteous rabbi, Rabbi Aryeh Levine. He went to Avraham and told him about the matter and asked him if he could help her. Even though he himself worked very hard to support himself, R'Avraham looked into the matter and found that she was short two and a half Mandatory Liras every month, and he would secretly send her this amount every month. She never knew the source of this money. This arrangement lasted for years.

Rabbi Aryeh Levine, who had interested himself in the situation, heard from her that she didn't know who this rescuing angel was, who sent her money each month so she could sustain herself. With great emotion R'Aryeh went to his brother-in-law, the Gaon rabbi of Jerusalem and said to him, "You should know, my dear brother-in-law, that your son Avraham, is a righteous man, a foundation of the world. He performs wondrous acts of kindness. I am humbled by all the kindnesses he does; would that I could merit to sit near him in the World of Truth, to fulfill the command of the prophet of God, "He has told you, O man, what is good and what the Lord requires of you: Only to do justice and to love goodness and to walk modestly with your God." (Micah 6:8)

R'Avraham is an offshoot of a family of wonderful Torah scholars, the great ones of their generation, the beloved son of the great Gaon, the rabbi of Jerusalem.

It is possible to use the verse in Parshat Mishpatim (Exod. 22:7) to describe him, "The master of the house shall come near to God." As explained by one of the Chassidic masters, the "master of the house, (a layman (בעל הבית)" that is neither a rabbi or a "holy vessel" [leader] can also draw near to God with his heart and all his soul.

Together with his devoted spouse, the wife of his youth, the good hearted and wise Malka, the daughter of Rabbi Yitzchak Jaffe, they have established a splendid home.

"In old age they still produce fruit; they are full of sap and freshness," (Ps. 92:15. May they merit much nachas from their beloved descendants, and may eternal joy rest upon them

Our Uncle Avraham Frank

By Zehava (Goldie) Bazak, daughter of Tanchum, Avraham's oldest brother

Each member of our expansive family has their own Uncle Avraham. Dod Avram, as we all called him, because we swallowed the letter Heh from the middle of his name, even though we all knew that the faith in Hashem was the basis of his existence, the simple and complete faith in Hashem, His Torah and His pathways. Each one of us, from the youngest to oldest, has a place with Dod Avram, all of us living in Zion and the rest of us living beyond the great sea.

Within my earliest memories, somewhere in the mists of childhood innocence, the figure of Dod Avram appears, a noble man, a young man like a cedar tree who symbolized, perhaps more than anything, the fundamental joy in being alive, a zest for life, simple, natural, true and vibrant, that overflows its banks and carries away everyone around him. The background of the family history is saturated with pain and loss, suffering and contending with the difficulties in the storms of life. The dimensions of sorrow and loss has been sharpened and plunged deeply into the depths of the soul to the extent that it could be hard to celebrate, from the aspect of "What is the point of joy?" That was precisely Dod Avram's contribution. Wherever he went he carried his simple joy with him, hope and faith which supports and strengthens the aspect of "How can a living being complain?"

"To always be joyous" is a level that very people are able to achieve, and it is especially tested during calamitous times that people face, heaven forbid, the difficult hours of bitter trials. Life caused Dod Avram to pass through these periods and he emerged from them all strengthened by the power of the faith that he imbibed along with his mother's milk, in the home of grandfather and grandmother. He accepted the decree without appeal, without question or complaint, and, by necessity, continued along the path despite it all, and remained faithful, grateful to God, joyous and good hearted.

As I have said, Dod Avram is intertwined in my memories of celebrating holidays in Grandfather's home; he is always embedded in memories of the Seder night, at the center of the long table, around which we all sat, at whose head was Grandfather in all of his glory, light and illumination spread across his face as he conducted the Seder quietly and meticulously. Around him are sons and daughters, sons-in-law and daughters-in-law, grandsons and granddaughters. The hours lengthen and eyelids slowly droop, sleepiness descends upon me and suddenly a mighty voice pierces the cobwebs of sleep, a booming voice that, as it were, raises heaven itself, "And it was at midnight" [ויהי בחצי הלילה], Dod Avram sweeping everyone away with a mighty song. A wide and warm smile spread across Grandfather's face, a smile of joy, the joy of celebrating the Seder as it should be done, according to all laws in their particulars, and faith in the eternal Jewish people.

Another memory from another holiday in the evening ending Hoshanah Rabbah [ushering in Simchat Torah], Dod Avram in Grandfather's house, excited and arousing the enthusiasm of the throng of visitors who gathered at the house, the worshippers from the Achva Synagogue, who came to greet Grandfather and accompany him all the way to the synagogue for Simchat Torah prayers. Every so often Dod Avram would pop the cork off bottles of beer and generously pour beer into glasses, and the joy, true joy, gripped everyone, and, with Dod Avram directing the song, the entire crowd set out on their way, joyously singing through the streets of the city. At their head marched Grandfather, patiently and with contained joy, and at his side and behind him the people were singing and chanting until they reached the synagogue. A fantastic and unforgettable spectacle.

Dod Avram was an original man in the way he blended his qualities. From his earliest days he was a man of work and labor, who fulfilled the verse, "When you earn your bread by the sweat of your brow, you will be happy and it will be good." (Ps. 128:2). He was a man of action who excelled in his personal integrity and the way he walked with God and man. Serving God came before any other task, and in every synagogue he attended he very quickly became a dominant and outstanding figure, always leading the prayers with strength and vigor, different traditions and melodies, part of the fabric of the synagogue's existence. This is the appropriate place to mention his special love for the world of cantorial music and to prayer leaders. He greatly enjoyed classical cantorial music and performances by outstanding cantors. With his strong and rich voice he could repeat without difficulty certain wonderful sections and these melodies added pleasure to every person who sat at Dod Avram's table with the mistress of the house, Dodah Malkah.

I well remember the wedding ceremony of Dod Avram and Dodah Malkah, a young bride beautiful and graceful

[נאה וחסודה] on the wide porch of Grandfather's house. The wedding celebration was held on the eve of Passover, very modestly, during the year of mourning after the death of Grandmother, may her memory be a blessing, against the backdrop of deep mourning in the wake of her passing. Dod Avram's marriage to Malkah brought him some measure of comfort, and in a wonderful partnership which is an example and model to us all, together built their household into an inviting and pleasant sanctuary for every family member in Israel and abroad. Malkah's contribution to the partnership is immeasurable, and together, they comprise a strong and united front.

For many decades he worked hard in the factory and the young manufacturing business. Many projects went through his hands, large and small. They included public and secret ones during the days of the underground opposed to the British Mandate in the Land of Israel. Dod Avram, a son of Jerusalem, who faithfully loved the nation of Israel, participated in the defense of our city and its inhabitants in the days of the "events" [מאורעות] which hit us wave upon wave. As a faithful patriot who believed wholeheartedly in the revival of Israel, he modestly made his contribution to its safety. Dod Avram was always completely prepared to address the needs of the house, creative in his work, and completely discreet. On many occasions he found appropriate solutions to difficult technical problems regarding armaments, ammunition and defense, but he never boasted about his creativity nor did he ever adorn himself with plumage for his professional accomplishments.

Dod Avram was an industrious man who arose early his entire life to serve the Creator, and he served God joyously. He went out to his labors every day, winter or summer, unwearied, without breaks, with energy, vigor and determination. I remember him on blazing and sticky hot summer nights in Tel Aviv, without air conditioning, when he would arrive at the house of Dodah Rachel, at the end of a crushing day of work, and he would be fresh, full of happiness, laughter and wit, as alert as it is were early in the morning, bursting with life, curiosity, with a thirst to learn new things, involved in all that was happening around him.

Dod Avram especially loved to share good news, and that's how I remember him from those bygone days, when there would be a delighted tap on the window pane in the wee hours of the morning, waking up the slumberers, telling of a new birth, a grandchild or a cousin. In the course of life, which is built on the sweet and bitter, he also had to, at times, convey difficult news.

Above all, Dod Avram was a dedicated family man who loved us and drew us close, joining us in times of joy just as in hours of sorrow and loss. Our Jewish calendar tends towards the holidays and celebrations, but there are also many yahrzeits of member of our wide branched family, who are no longer with us, to the sorrow of our hearts. Avram continued to enliven them to protect their memories, he joins with all of us, circling back and forth in the alleyways of the cemetery, whatever date on the calendar, without regard for his comfort. All of this flows from the foundation of goodness upon which his personality is built, the foundation of giving to the other, giving of oneself in every way possible, whether actual acts of loving-kindness, whether true acts of loving-kindness [towards the deceased חסד של אמת], giving secretly or openly, whether directly or indirectly, one could always recruit Dod Avram to any helpful project which is required.

In addition to all this, Dod Avram was a treasure trove of stories from the past. He recalls clearly and with clarity events, figures and images from the past and is an untapped source that casts light on distant times.

He loved and greatly venerated our father, R' Tanchum, his older brother. He always tried to help him as much as possible. It is no surprise that in the photos of my wedding to Moshe, Dod Avram accompanies us to the chuppah along with our fathers.

When he returned to live in Jerusalem, after residing in Tel Aviv for many years, father ztz"l was no longer alive. Dod Avram considered it a privilege to take it upon himself to help our invalid sister, Esther, z"l and our brother-in-law R' Yosef ztz"l, as much as possible, going to their home at a set time, volunteering to help with any errand or whatever assistance, despite the constraints on his time, with a desire to somewhat ease their difficult and extended suffering.

And so we find in Dod Avram a rare combination of a proud and upright Jew on one hand, and an extremely humble man on the other hand. A true man, without any posturing, never pretending to be anything other than himself, expressing himself with integrity, truth and genuine respect. His wonderful sense of humor and his skill with gematria [where Hebrew letters are used as a numerical value to create connections between words and phrases] provided us with many moments of unbridled laughter, a knowing and satirical glance, an unusual point of view, a reflection of the reality of our lives. He is a whole hearted paragon, rejoicing in each of our accomplishments and wishing us only good things. Together with Malkah they interwove a wonderful system of relationship, easily connecting with every one of the family, at any age, so that their home became a destination for pilgrimage, which was always accompanied by tasty aromas that wafted from Malkah's kitchen; a well-tended home, always fresh and shining, inviting in all who are in need of royal hospitality.

Dod Avram is deeply disappointed with our current state of affairs; he did not believe that matters would come to this. Even so, he continues along his optimistic path, maintaining hope in a better future. We are blessed to have him and may the pleasantness of God (Ps. 90:17) be upon him and Malkah until 120.

Pages of a Book

By Raffi Frank, son of Avraham and Malkah

I was happy for this opportunity to add a few words to this book. There are emotions that accompany you for many years but you lack the right and appropriate platform to express them. Anyone who knows Abba knows that any word you may say about him would be met by a glance of surprise, as if this doesn't apply to him, and this be accompanied by a slight chuckle and sparkling eyes that portray confusion. With him, humility is not in word only and on the exterior, nor is it a sort of "pride in humility," I refer to those who only try to make themselves appear humble, but who, in truth, seek glory and honor. With Abba the humility is true and honest. This matter also appropriately inter-meshes with another aspect that we find in him—he is a truthful man. He never did anything to merely curry favor in the eyes of others, but only ever acted according to truth.

Even when he came to tell future generations about the land of Israel in the 20th century by telling his life story, he did not deviate from his manner of minimizing his actions and sticking to the truth. It is very hard for writers of history to adhere to this approach. Each person has his point of view about reality, and certainly regarding history. The personality and the character of the writer are the bases of his writing. It's bad enough that we can open our most up to date communication devices, and see how each person presents his reality as he sees it, and it appears that on each device you see a different reality. And if these things are true regarding what we see today, how much more so regarding things from the past.

However, despite what was said above, there is one thing about which Abba lacks objectivity, regarding the land of Israel. The Torah speaks of Yaakov who flees from Esav, that he folded up the land of Israel and placed it under his head [midrash]. This always amazed me; how could such a thing be possible that one could all of the land, fold it up and place it under one man's head, and I thought it could only be a fable. However, anyone who is familiar with Abba, and knows his true love for the land of Israel, as one who was privileged to be born in it and never leave it, can sense how his entire life was devoted to loving the land, and can understand the significance of this idea, how it is possible that the entire land of Israel could be folded up and placed under one man's head.

And if the story of his life is the story of the land of Israel, we have to another perspective. There were three patriarchs of the Israelite people, and it was not in vain that the faith of Israel was formed from the characteristics of its patriarchs. Each one of them left his mark in a certain area, and only the integration of the three of them created the infrastructure of the nation of Israel. Pirkei Avot begins with a quotation of R' Shimon HaTzadik, "The world rests upon three things: Torah, service, and deeds of kindness." These three foundation upon which the world rests, correspond to the three things that the patriarchs impressed upon the nature of the nation: Avraham—the characteristic of kindness; Yitzchak—who exemplified service; Yaakov—Torah.

All of his acquaintances and friends [a play on words, מכיריו ומוקיריו], and there are many, will immediately discern that these three foundations which characterized the patriarchs are also concealed within Abba.

Avraham, "The name is fitting for you and you are well fitted to your name." (שמך נאה לך ואתה נאה לשמך) שמך נאה לך from the Rosh Hashanah liturgy). Just seeing the delight flashing from his eyes you see the goodness of his heart. I recall a time when we were walking along the street and a stranger approached, someone he'd never seen before, and simply said, without any introduction, "I can see from the look in your eyes that you are a man with a good heart." Many people can testify to the truth of that statement. He is always the very first to help and assist anyone in need. He did this without seeking compensation, while attempting to minimize his actions. Inviting guests, visiting the sick, accompanying the dead [for burial] were just part of his life. Not only notable guests, but there were many downtrodden people who frequently ate at his table. There is almost no yahrzeit among those near and far when he did not visit their grave. Whether it was strict observance on the memorial day of his nephews of the Kaplan family, or family members from abroad who were buried in the dust of Israel.

Yitzchak, although the intentions of the sages was service, in regard to the sacrificial service, we can also understand the matter according to the simple meaning of the text. He is identified with the work of his hands with which he labored and toiled for a great many years. He invested most of his talents into this. I can attest that the joy of creativity never left him. He saw the manual labor as an intellectual challenge and he did valiantly. The engineers from the military industries revered him, that a man without any academic training was able to solve complicated problems for them. What a happy day it was for him when he was able to design the spring from twisted wires for the Mirage planes, after the French had placed an embargo on bringing them to Israel. And he was even happier at the fact that his creation brought even better results than the French made ones. He wasn't named "The King of Springs" for nothing! He invested himself in this manual labor. There were times when things were tough, due to a recession or other reasons. I used to say that those in the know could discern his mood from the angle of his legendary flat cap that he always wore at work. How appropriate was definition of a spring, "a lively inanimate object." I remember the times I worked at the plant during vacation and tried to make a spring, Abba said: "A curled iron thread is not a spring."

With wisdom and intelligence he turned work with metal materials into a spiritual creation. When it was time for payment for the results, he was embarrassed and bewildered to seek compensation. In the house there was an atmosphere that money was almost in the same category as a vulgar word. You managed with little, and no extras. I don't recall a single time that we went on vacation, excursions within Israel, yes, but to travel in order to do nothing, just like that, to relax, would be considered a complete waste of time.

In these efforts he also recognized the challenge of Zionism and felt that he was contributing for the sake of the land of Israel. He preferred to work on behalf of Israel's security and earn less, than to work in the private sector. It was very difficult in the later years, when authorities began to make demands and asked that he bring a permit from the technical institute. He could not be reconciled to the fact that someone would critique his work, in the profession of which he was a member.

And if we are dealing with Yitzchak, we must add on prayer. For in these days there is no holy temple and instead of the sacrificial service the sages established prayer, as "Instead of bulls we will pay [the offering of] our lips" (Hosea 14:3). Prayer is the service of the heart. This is yet another layer in his life. His prayer was like counting coins word by word. Prayer that was full of feeling and infused with faith and nearness to the Creator. There was also the administrative side of prayer—being a gabbai (manager of prayer services), which he carried with wisdom, great tact and knowledge. He was beloved and accepted by all the worshippers at the Bilu Synagogue in Tel Aviv, which was, under his management, at the height of its glory and splendor.

Yaakov—the pillar of Torah. The glorious figure, was the foundation of the house, was grandfather, R'Zvi Pesach Frank. Not a day passed when his name was not mentioned, or some story about him, about his behavior and his personality. What yearning, love and reverence did he feel for him—it is impossible to describe. Today, now that he has retired from work, I see the many hours he spends following a set plan of study.

The three foundations of the world: Torah, service and performing acts of loving kindness which were the characteristics of the patriarchs: Avraham, Yitzchak and Yaakov are also within him.

Another characteristic of Abba is his sense of humor, which often includes a quick tongue and sharpness. These days he has reached 89 years (פ"ט)—may he live to be 120—and honed his tongue to say, "I've returned to being a boy in childhood (טף). When he'd see a Jew driving on Shabbat he would mutter under his breath in Yiddish, "There goes a

Jew," which has two meanings, a Jew travels and even so he is a Jew. In Tel Aviv the neighbors used to wash their cars on Shabbat. He characterize this as "The glory of the auto on Shabbat" [a play on words תפארת" "אוטו" ליום השבת]. I've brought only a few examples; were we to include them we could publish a wonderful book on his word play.

I would be remiss if I don't add his never ending involvement in anything going on in the country. Listening to the news every half hour, his eyes looking at the television, a transistor radio in his hand and his ears listening to the news. Always the same responses to the haters of Israel especially within the members of the nation who bring destruction upon the people of Israel. For fifty years now it's been, "We're lost!" He'd get angry and rage against those who destroy the religion and raise the battle flag against those who uphold the Torah. Fundamentally, he directed his anger against the Supreme Court and its post Zionist ideology, turning Israel into a secular democratic state, and the nation of Israel into a nation like all other nations.

Everything described above and count not have existed without Imma, the industrious, the talented and the intellectual, who was always "The shade on your right hand," (Ps. 121), All of the acts of kindness would not have happened without her. Their partnership arouses admiration. Imma complements Abba in those areas of household management he doesn't touch. Her devotion to Abba and towards all who surround her is renowned and glorious. She never needs anything, with any pain or uncomfortable feeling, ""this will pass," "nothing happened." She is so energetic that even if you want to, it's impossible to help her. I remember years ago, after a traffic accident in Tel Aviv, when a truck ran a red light and hit Abba's car and

Imma's shoulder was broken. They tried to bring help into the house, but the maid quit after one day, feeling herself superfluous. Her day begins much earlier than the roosters crow. Her only indulgences are a steaming hot bath or reading a good book in French or English, not her native language, of course, but nothing translated. She is always in action, seeking contentment, amazing cleanliness and outstanding order. If one were to open the clothes closet, with permission of course, you'd clearly see how things stand, the linens, the fragrance that wafts from the clothes would sense the perfection we are talking about. Abundant food, amazingly tasty, with spicy seasoning, pickled and brined, the quintessential taste of the land of Israel. Pastries unlike those from any other source. She would never be unprepared to welcome guests for a meal. There are many domains where she is incomparable, the keeper of the house (עקרת הבית) plain and simple. Whoever would hear her singing Hallel of Milevsky (?) at the Passover Seder, together with Abba, listening to the harmony in their voices can sense this characterization. Modesty and humility are a part of it, she would always say, "What will they say about me, that I was a Berye? [an outstanding home maker]" She doesn't believe that people say much more than this about her these days. If they called him "king," then it is fitting that she be called the "queen" (Malkah), "queen of the home."

At the beginning of the Torah portion of Lech Lecha, the verse reads, "I will make you into a great nation, and I will bless you and I will make your name great." (Gen. 12:2), Rashi quotes the sages in Tractate Pesachim (117b) [discussing the first paragraph of the Amidah, the blessing of the patriarchs]:

"I will make of you a great nation" this is the verse that teaches us that we say in the first blessing "the God of Abraham," "And I will bless you," is the verse that teaches us that we say also in the first blessing, "the God of Yitzchak," "And I will make your name great," is the verse that teaches us that we also say in the first blessing, "the God of Yaakov." Could we not conclude the blessing by mentioning all of them? The Torah therefore continues "And be a blessing," which explains why we conclude the blessing with you, Avraham, and not mention all three.

The Avot blessing concludes with "Magen Avraham," (protector of Israel). Just as the Holy One Blessed Be He promised Avraham that his descendants would continue his legacy, so let us lift up our prayers to God that our offspring will carry on the legacy and immerse themselves in Torah, Service and deeds of loving kindness.

With great and eternal love, with praise honor and respect

Rafi and Aliza

With Great Love

*By Gitti Yardeni,
daughter of Avraham and
Malkah Frank*

When Dani and I urged Abba to put into writing the wonderful stories he'd tell us from time to time, he would always avoid it. As one who knows his nature I knew that the main cause of this is the delicate nature of his soul, his humility and modesty. This is also the reason that I write this. Now that it is finally complete, I read the manuscript and the outstanding fact is that he, essentially, speaks of others, when we intended that he speak of himself.

So, for example he doesn't speak of his appearance as a youth, although the photographs speak for themselves and show a good looking man with a sturdy handsome physique. He was, as our "younger" speakers would say, a "looker" (חתיך). As far as I know, he himself never admitted to his good looks and the impression he made on "the fairer sex."

I remember him as a young, hardworking father, leaving early in the morning while it was still dark, walking to the spring factory on
Derech Petach Tikvah, returning at noon on his "funny looking" bicycle, quickly eating the meal that Imma had prepared, then returning to work in the plant until he returned home late in the evening, often after we were asleep in our beds.

And it is impossible to write about Abba without Imma. Abba's tenderness and good heart completely meshed with

Imma's good heart and sacrifice. The connection between them created a couple that was beloved by all those who know them. Each one had a specific task within their partnership, with much mutual support. When Imma would go to the hairdresser and Abby would be home waiting for her, he would, in his joking way, say he couldn't be sure he'd recognize her when she came home. Abba knew how to tell a joke, and when, and to whom. I remember when he'd say, with a smile, to plug my ears when I was still a young girl and he'd tell a joke that wasn't "kosher" for his daughter's ears. His sense of humor was accompanied by a sensitive and empathetic soul. I remember when we celebrated the Passover Seder in grandfather's house and we were young children, very disappointed that we didn't see the prophet Elijah, and all of a sudden Abba pops up with a funny hat and a scarf over his face and announced that the prophet Elijah had appeared. The laughter that greeted his appearance completely raised our spirits.

The good hearts of Abba and Imma, together and separately, are a model of loving the person as a person, and to help and be considerate of others. What the one lacks, the other supplies. Their consideration of others was incalculable and served for us as an example and model. They are always the first to visit the sick, to accompany the dead, to provide funds for the needy. These were the values we were raised with at home. Their nobility and greatness of spirit were also seen when sorrow and catastrophe befell our family, the inner circle as well as the greater circle.

Abba and Imma hosted many people in their home and still do today. Some of them had more than a meal. Sometimes their hosting lasted weeks, months and even years, and always with Imma's full heart and strength. We usually had guests for Shabbat meals, relatives, friends and even friends of friends. I recall one meal in our home when we hosted the United States ambassador to Israel at the time, Walworth Barbour with his (Jewish) wife, who was related to our neighbors. In addition to the abundant delicacies that Imma prepared, they participated along with the Shabbat songs that Abba and Imma sang with their strong and beautiful voices, which contributed to the atmosphere. Many times, after services in the Bilu synagogue, where he served for many years as gabbai, Abba brought home guests or worshippers whose loneliness he sensed.

Their friendly relationships exemplified their wide social connections. Their friends came from every sector of society, religious and secular, and every hue on the political spectrum. These friendships have been maintained over the course of many years.

Despite his easy going nature, he would not tolerate anyone attacking my honor. During summer vacation I would come to the plant to help out in the office, alongside his legendary secretary, Yonah. One day after work Abba came home and said that unfamiliar young man had come to his office in the plant boasting, "Last night I went out dancing with your daughter." Abba, as Yonah described it, opened the cabinet, pulled out a knife he had just that day bought for Imma from some peddler and threatened the stunned young man, "Get out of here or I will cut you!" The young man fled for his life. I will add that during the investigation Abba conducted when he came home, it was revealed that I had actually been home with him and Imma. It took a long time for us to recover from the laughter that seized us. By the way, I never discovered who that poor young man was. This story testifies to Abba's protective nature. The minute you start talking about his offspring he turns into a "roaring lion."

There is an aspect of Abba of which I am sure many do not know, which is his intuitive understanding of art. He revealed such an interesting artistic taste that many times I have felt it a pity that he never had structured training in the subject. Imma, in her own way as well, did not rest on her accomplishments. At a relatively advanced age, in between her work as a home maker, raising and caring for the house and family, hosting friends and relatives and feeding them (I remember a period when Imma would prepare a gigantic pot of fruit soup that she would simmer until evening), Imma learned French and she reads it and is fluent in that language.

The love that they give to all who know them comes right back to them. Many friends and acquaintances consider them model parents and I have heard from a few that they'd be willing to be adopted. The mutual love between them, towards their offspring, surpasses the constraints of age and they have close relationships with their grandchildren and great grandchildren.

I know that some will say that I am prejudiced, and that is certainly true. But I love them with all my soul—every word I have written is completely true.

Glossary

Agunah—A woman who is "anchored" in a marriage if her husband is missing or refuses to divorce her
Aliyah—1) Being called up to the Torah during services; 2) moving to the land of Israel
Aron Kodesh—Holy ark that holds the Torah scrolls
Beit Din—Jewish court
Beit Midrash—A study hall
Bimah—Platform where the prayer reader stands
Brit Milah—Ritual circumcision
Challah—Bread traditionally baked for Shabbat and holidays
Chalukah—The charity system that gathered funds to support the impoverished Jewish community in Israel
Chametz—Food that is forbidden to be eaten on Passover because it is leavened
Charedi—Someone who follows very strict religious practice.
Chassidism—A movement that grew in the Jewish community of eastern Europe in the 18th century which emphasized spirituality and mysticism
Chavruta—A study partner
Chevra Kaddisha—Burial society
Cholent—A traditional stew often prepared for Shabbat
Chumash—The five books of Moses
Chuppah—Marriage canopy
Daven—pray
Dayan—Judge
Din Torah—A judicial pronouncement from a Jewish court
Dod—Uncle
Dodah—Aunt
Eshet Chayil—A woman of valor
Gabbai—Manager of synagogue services

Gaon—Genius

Gareen—Literally, "kernel." Also refers to a nucleus of young settlers

Gemara—Aramaic component of the Talmud

Get—The Jewish divorce decree

Haftarah—An additional reading from the prophets read after the Torah portion on Shabbat and holidays

Haganah—Defense organization in Israel before the establishment of the state

Haggadah—The traditional book recited and studied on Passover

Halacha—The system of Jewish law

Kaddish—A prayer often recited by a mourner

Kasher—Make a utensil kosher

Khan—An inn

Kibbutz—Collective settlement

Kiddush—Blessing over wine to welcome Shabbat and holidays

Kiddush Hashem—An act that brings honor to God's name

Knesset—Gathering; Israel's parliament

Kol Koreh—General announcement or call to action

Kollel/Kollelim—An organization that provides stipends to students studying Talmud

Kreplach—Small dumplings

Lechi—Acronym for Lochamei Cherut Yisrael, a paramilitary organization in pre-state Israel

Maariv—Evening prayers

Maggid—A preacher

Matza—Unleavened bread eaten on Passover

Megillah—A scroll, often particularly referring to the book of Esther

Middot—Good personal characteristics

Mikvah—Ritual bath

Mitnagid—A member of a movement opposed to Chassidism

Mitzvah—Religious commandment

Palmach—The elite strike force of the Haganah

Pikuach Nefesh—The concept that one is required to break Jewish

law in order to save a life
Posek/Poskim—Rabbinic legal decisor
Rabbanit/Rebbetsin—Rabbi's wife
Sabra—A native of Israel, a cactus fruit
Sandek—The person given the honor of holding the baby during the circumcision
Savta—Grandmother
Shacharit—Morning prayers
Shamash—Caretaker of a synagogue
Sheva Brachot—The seven blessings recited at a wedding and for a week of festivities following a wedding
Shochet—A ritual slaughterer
Shul—Synagogue
Sofer—Scribe who writes a Torah scroll and other ritual texts
Sukkah—A booth built for the holiday of Sukkot
Tallit—Tallis, prayer shawl
Tzedakah—Charity
Yekke—A German Jew (typically very precise and orderly)
Yeshiva—A school dedicated to high level Talmud study
Yibbum—The ancient practice of a man marrying his brother's widow if there were no children from that marriage.
Yiddishkeit—Traditional Jewish practices
Yishuv/ Old Yishuv—Refers to the community of Jews who lived in Israel during the Ottoman Era
Yom Tov—A festival

www.ingramcontent.com/pod-product-compliance
Lightning Source LLC
LaVergne TN
LVHW041759060526
838201LV00046B/1051